Monteverdi in Venice

Monteverdi in Venice

Denis Stevens

Madison • Teaneck
Fairleigh Dickinson University Press
London: Associated University Presses

Associated University Presses
440 Forsgate Drive
Cranbury, NJ 08512

Associated University Presses
16 Barter Street
London WC1A 2AH, England

Associated University Presses
P.O. Box 338, Port Credit
Mississauga, Ontario
Canada L5G 4L8

The paper used in this publication meets the requirements of the American National Standard for Permanence of Paper for Printed Library Materials Z39.48-1984.

Library of Congress Cataloging-in-Publication Data

Stevens, Denis, 1922–
    Monteverdi in Venice / Denis Stevens.
        p.   cm.
    Includes bibliographical references (p.   ) and index.
    ISBN 0-8386-3879-1 (alk. paper)
    1. Monteverdi, Claudio, 1567–1643. 2. Composers—Italy—Biography.
I. Title.
ML410.M77 S79   2001
782'.0092—dc21
[B]   00-034766

PRINTED IN THE UNITED STATES OF AMERICA

to the memory of my parents
William and Edith Stevens
and of my Accademia friends
Ursula Connors, Edgar Fleet,
John Frost, Leslie Fyson, and
Yehudi Menuhin

Other works by Denis Stevens

The Mulliner Book
Thomas Tomkins
Tudor Church Music
A History of Song
The Letters of Claudio Monteverdi
Musicology in Practice
The Joy of Ornamentation
Early Music
Monteverdi: Songs and Madrigals
Monteverdi: Sacred, Secular, and Occasional Music

Contents

Illustrations

Preface

A new volume of Monteverdi studies by Denis Stevens is a welcome event: he has played a leading rôle in the consolidation and intensification of critical exegesis of the composer's work and life, following on the revival of enthusiasm for Monteverdi in the first part of the twentieth century. As musician and conductor, as well as musicologist, Denis Stevens has produced standard editions of the *Vespers,* of *Il Combattimento di Tancredi e Clorinda,* and other works, and—under the aegis of the Accademia Monteverdiana founded by him several decades ago—conducted numerous performances, including broadcasts in several countries of many of Monteverdi's extant works. His editions have purified earlier editions, particularly of notational misunderstandings, thereby establishing the most reliable scores.

His remarkable command of the intricacies of late Renaissance, and particularly North Italian linguistic usage has been the basis for his standard English edition of *The Letters of Claudio Monteverdi,* a volume interspersed with copious biographical and historical commentaries that make it an indispensable reference work for all students of the life and work of the composer (first edition London, Faber & Faber, 1980; second revised edition Oxford University Press, 1996). In the domain of iconography, Denis Stevens has in his latest publications clarified questions of authenticity relating to portraits of Monteverdi. And he has recently given us a volume of English versions of all madrigal texts set by Monteverdi that will be an essential companion for all performers of that unique and celebrated part of the composer's oeuvre.

—ALBI ROSENTHAL

Acknowledgments

Thanks are due to the Fondazione Claudio Monteverdi for kindly permitting an English translation of the essay on Monteverdi's *Selva morale e spirituale* (chapter 2) that appears in a different form in their edition of the 1640 publication.

I am grateful to copyright owners of the various photographs included. In many cases the name of the photographer could not be traced, but should it come to light, an acknowledgment will be made in any future edition of this book.

I wish to thank John Blackley and Barbara Lachman for their assistance in editing the text, also Christine Retz, my editor at Associated University Presses, for her thoughtful concern and expertise.

I also acknowledge permission to reprint or modify the material in chapter 3 (*Musical Times*) and chapter 6 (*Musical Quarterly*). Finally, I thank the Biblioteca Nazionale di San Marco, Venice, for permission to reproduce *Fiori Poetici*.

Much of the music discussed in this book is available through the website under the following reference: www:scholaantiqua.net. Performances are by the Accademia Monteverdiana (Denis Stevens); compact discs are listed, along with individual titles.

Monteverdi in Venice

1

Monteverdi: A Personal Approach

LIKE SO MANY *Monteverdi enthusiasts, I was first beguiled by hearing some of the music committed to disc by Nadia Boulanger and her group in 1937. In the following year she brought them to London where they gave a musical soirée at Lady Cunard's home. Beecham was present and heard, probably for the first time, excerpts from Books 7* (Concerto) *and 8* (Madrigali guerrieri ed amorosi) *by the Italian composer of three centuries before.*

I had just finished compiling a book on *The Rudiments of Orchestration,* carefully written in red and blue ink with text on the lined pages of an exercise book and musical examples on the plain pages. At sixteen I had never heard of Monteverdi, but as war clouds lowered I caught a glimpse of things to come on hearing a broadcast of one of Nadia Boulanger's records. They proved somewhat elusive in record shops, but I slowly assembled the five precious discs and then began to look for scores. By chance the RAF posted me to London, almost on the doorstep of the British Museum, and by slightly falsifying my age I was admitted to the North Library which then served as a wartime reading room. Malipiero's edition, although still incomplete, nevertheless provided the scores I needed.

Returning to Oxford in 1947 I saw the dark spines of two paperback music editions in a High Street bookstore. No title was visible: only the cryptic legend "VIII/1" and "VIII/2." I had accidentally

18 MONTEVERDI IN VENICE

found a copy of the late Venetian madrigals and occasional pieces in a Viennese edition reprinted from the Italian one. Overjoyed, I shared this treasure trove with members of a string quartet, but could not then introduce them to the joys of Monteverdian harmonies under the fingers. I recall gasps of astonishment, however, when they listened to the chaconne *Zefiro torna* performed by Cuénod and Derenne. I never dreamed that in a few years I would meet Hugues Cuénod in my daily round as senior producer of early music on the BBC Third Programme.

Less still did I guess that in a dozen years I would meet Nadia herself and ask her blessing on a Monteverdi enterprise that would encompass research, performance, and publication. Her fellow Trustees in the Accademia Monteverdiana were Yehudi Menuhin and Igor Stravinsky, and their messages testify to the support they gave throughout their lives. Yehudi (Lord Menuhin) had asked for my collaboration in a series of experimental recordings at the EMI Studios in January 1959, and a gracious gift from him—a facsimile of Bach's solo violin music to which he had written a Preface—launched a long and fruitful friendship. Exceptionally fortunate in

Letter from Nadia Boulanger

2. The Grove,
Highgate Village,
London, N.6.

19th December, 1960.

Denis Stevens, Esq.,
41 Blenheim Park Road,
South Croydon,
Surrey.

Dear Denis,

      Thank you for your letter of the 14th December.
An excellent idea - I am honoured to accept your
invitation to be Vice-President of the Accademia
Monteverdiana.   On the other hand, I do not feel entitled to this until I have identified myself with Monteverdi by playing some of his works.

      Perhaps I shall fulfil my duties in reverse,
by joining the Accademia and then giving evidence of
my merit!

                Devotedly,

Note from Yehudi Menuhin

my friends and professional contacts, I lost no time in developing
the Monteverdi connection.

    Some of my ambitions developed slowly, for Claudio was some-
times pushed aside to make way for my studies in English music
(*The Worcester Fragments* and *Music in Honor of St Thomas of
Canterbury,* to name but two), and I rapidly learned that projects
take up far more time and money than I thought possible. Each of
the two just mentioned took twenty-five years, and could not even

have been begun before I had photographed all the musical manuscripts in color (now at Princeton University Library). Working on the principle of *nihil humani alienum a me puto,* I also began a photographic archive of Monteverdi's letters copied from originals in Mantua, Florence, Rome, Paris, and Oxford.

My abiding belief in the validity of performance planted ideas whose fruit would not be tasted for as many as forty years (in the literal, not Biblical sense), for I became a member of the Garrick Club in 1957, one year after Yehudi Menuhin joined that gregarious crowd of literary, legal and theatrical gentlemen. I resolved to perform, one day, a few minutes of Monteverdi's music on the club premises, and the wish became true when a members' lift was installed in the mid-1990s. At the inaugural ceremony we invited a brass group to perform cheerful music capable of being heard above the din of conversation and the conversation of dinner. Among the music sheets, I planted the thrice-repeated Toccata from *Orfeo.* The music that provided a lift for Mantuan spirits in 1607 celebrated a lift for Garrick members nearly four centuries later.

Orfeo was my first major production on the Third Programme. Two live broadcasts were planned for June 1952. I, who until then had cheerfully realized continuo parts on paper, sadly and suddenly realized that I had a major problem on my hands. But Walter Goehr, the designated conductor, agreed at once with my intention to reveal Monteverdi's hidden rhythmic subtleties, while I supported his plan to supplement the orchestration of the last three acts. Anyone who has studied the composer's life at the Mantuan court between 1604 and 1608 will have seen that they were years of unbelievable stress and strain ending in severe illness. If Monteverdi began his operatic task in earnest enthusiasm, pressures of one kind or another—not least of all the approaching deadline—obliged him merely to sketch out an orchestration that had in the beginning shown immense variety and resource. The decision to amplify was therefore just and necessary.

Never having heard a note of *Orfeo,* I went to the Gramophone Library and listened to the only extant recording, that of the Argentine-born Max Reger pupil, Ferruccio Calusio, issued by Italian HMV in 1939.

I was frankly horrified by what I heard. At the beginning of act 2 a vague, unmetricized pseudo-mysterious meandering pervaded my ears, yet this Sinfonia foreshadows Orfeo's "I am coming back to you, dear woods and sea-shores," demanding an up-beat feeling of

CLAUDIO MONTEVERDI

ORFEO

Transcribed by Gian Francesco Malipiero
edited by Walter Goehr

*Decoration from the title-page
of the original edition of* 1609

La Musica Prologo	Alfred Deller	*(counter-tenor)*
Orfeo	Pierre Bernac	*(baritone)*
Messagiera	Irma Kolassi	*(soprano)*
Euridice	Ilse Wolf	*(soprano)*
Speranza	Jennifer Vyvyan	*(soprano)*
Ninfa		
Caronte	Norman Walker	*(bass)*
Proserpina	Mary Jarred	*(contralto)*
Plutone	Martin Lawrence	*(bass)*
Apollo	Bruce Boyce	*(baritone)*

Shepherds and spirits sung by
Raymond Nilsson *(tenor)*
Wilfred Brown *(tenor)*
Norman Platt *(baritone)*

BBC CHORUS
(Chorus-Master, Leslie Woodgate)

An Orchestra conducted by
WALTER GOEHR

Repetiteur, George Coop

PRODUCED BY DENIS STEVENS
Studio I, Maida Vale

Radio Times billing of *Orfeo*

happiness and recognition. But there *was* no up-beat to the thinly-disguised hemiola pattern, obscured in the first instance by the "barring" of the original printed edition and followed slavishly by all other revisions from Eitner (1881) to D'Indy (1905), Orefice (1909), Malipiero (1923), Westrup (1925), Orff (1931), and Benvenuti 1 and 2 (1934; 1942).

Concluding that the main point had been missed, I reached for a pencil and drew bar-lines through the score to indicate the correct accents. As I listened and drew, it became clear that vital questions of meter had been totally ignored by a succession of musicologists and "editors" over the previous eighty years!

The source of their main mental quagmire derived from a sheepish pursuit of printed "bar-lines," instead of the true and correct meter, in every challenging passage that passed before their eyes. Rather than find the music behind the notes, they had discovered (as the composer said in one of his letters) "only the shadow, but not the substance." The examples below are but two of many (and from Monteverdi alone of many), omitting the countless contemporaneous composers who shared his style and technical equipment.

Thirty-five years after that broadcast, a handbook about *Orfeo* appeared under John Whenham's editorship. Although the book conveys much, it is perhaps significant that the one production that reached the greatest number of connoisseurs (BBC 1952) was barely mentioned. The people contributing to the book were too young to know what had happened.

This, briefly, is the story. Walter Goehr, Jeremy Noble, and I made hundreds of significant changes in meter and texture, as a result of which the musical world registered praise, approval and enthusiasm. An early-music man came to my office and asked to borrow the score. Somewhat against my better judgment I handed it over—and never saw it again. But what I did see and hear a few years later was a recorded and published edition of *Orfeo* based on the score he had taken away. None of the editors was acknowledged or thanked.

This kind of editorial tumescence can also be seen in the handbook's chapter by Jane Glover, who tells us (in an essay written c. 1984) that "Orfeo's *Ecco pur,* barred in 4/2, is actually in 3/2 and begins on the upbeat."

But this and many other solutions I had already discovered in 1952, more than three decades previously, and had published in the Novello edition of 1967, which Glover had clearly seen since she

A passage from *Orfeo* in the 1930 edition and in the 1967 edition

mentions it several times. The musical example on Whenham's p. 148 copies exactly what had appeared 20 years earlier on p. 40 of the Novello edition! The same is equally true of other passages.

Even today I continue to see "editions" of operas, madrigals and motets whose music has been squeezed into iron four-four-bar cages when the true meter is quite otherwise. If editors and teachers perpetrate such violence on the music, what shall their pupils do?

At a BBC live broadcast in November 1993, a member of the panel asked whether, "as one of the leading British Monteverdi scholars," I would not agree that great strides had been made since those early days. "Yes," I answered, "BACKWARDS!" Not only was I never allowed to broadcast again, but my existing talks on

Monteverdi had the specially-chosen musical examples ripped out and, without consulting me, replaced by other interpretations that made nonsense of the script. It is this small-mindedness that makes broadcasting such a hazard nowadays.

But 1952 was indeed another age. I produced one live broadcast every week, and also had charge of late-night repeat recordings of chamber music both vocal and instrumental. Every large-scale production had to be "live," since orchestral recording was rarely permitted. Readers interested in the situation as it then was should sample Humphrey Carpenter's engaging book *The Envy of the World.*

We had good administrators, some of whom showed sympathy and understanding for the early music idiom and encouraged outside broadcasts from abbeys, collegiate chapels, and historic homes. My innate feeling for our history and culture enabled me to develop a long-range collaboration with the various domestic and overseas programs, and with European and Transcription services. My links with senior management, although strong and friendly, were never better than in Sir William Glock's time. He loved Monteverdi and invited me to give the first concert of his music in the framework of the Proms, for which I drew on an ensemble of twelve singers and four instrumentalists.

*   *   *

Some time afterwards, on my 60th birthday, Glock recalled those years in a letter that formed a part of my unpublished "Festschrift":

> This is to send you warmest greetings from myself and Anne for your birthday. I have always admired you as a great musicologist and also for being a nonconformist, an iconoclast, and equally for passionately believing in the value of music-making and not just of study alone.

For me, music-making and research were never separated, for the one seemed to feed the other. A few days in a great library would inspire me with sufficient material to launch a whole series of programs, and these would at once demand conversion into a new musical experience.

It was the same with theory and practice. Bibliography and translation posed their peculiar problems, which I enjoyed trying to solve, but there were many others to be attended to in the music

itself. At certain times I felt as if I were moving at an almost un-
comfortable speed between study and concert hall, and when I
woke up it was invariably to find myself in a taxi. Dr. H. C. Robbins
Landon came to this conclusion:

> What I have always particularly admired about your work is your un-
> canny ability to wed the theoretical with the practical, in both of which
> fields you are supremely gifted. What should one admire more, that
> flawless edition of the Monteverdi letters or your flawless performance
> of a Monteverdi "Gloria"—or indeed an Irish folksong-setting by Bee-
> thoven?

My final year on the staff of the BBC saw the beginning of a
lengthy period of casual collaboration, bringing my total period of
service, on and off the staff, to 46 years. It was during 1966 that I
was called on to prepare a series of Monteverdi programs for the
400th anniversary of his birth. I looked long and hard in the exten-
sive BBC music library for new repertoire of the highest standard.
In my own library the old collected edition supplemented by Osthoff's volume proved a good starting point, but I was anxious to
track down many unfamiliar compositions.

In fact it was the work mentioned by Robbins Landon that revealed a considerable lacuna in the performing material. The *Gloria*
for seven voice-parts, as far as I could gather, had never been broadcast at all. A card-index entry listed the work, but without further
indication of a bag containing chorus and orchestral material. I set
about to remedy this by drawing on my notes from Vogel's massive
essay and inventory (*Vierteljahrsschrift für Musikwissenschaft,*
1887), where there is a note about the performance of this masterpiece with "trombe squarciate."

Using the orchestration indicated by Monteverdi's rubrics and by
the Venetian description given by Vogel, I prepared an edition that
we rehearsed at St. Paul's Knightsbridge and recorded during the
last week of August 1966 for Transcription Service. It was in fact
the very first modern performance, and the assembled Accademia
Monteverdiana greeted it with resounding applause.

A kind of Monteverdi madness then ensued, each choral director
vying with the other to put on these stunning but hitherto unknown
works. One man rushed to a recording company while another trav-
eled around the festivals. Delighted at first, even though nobody
had sought my co-operation, I noticed the BBC bags emptied time

and time again. I returned to New York, happy enough to have
started yet another wave of enthusiasm for the Cremonese giant.

Next year, however, was not so easy. When I wanted to borrow
the parts I had caused to be made, the whole of the *Gloria* bag had
been whisked off somewhere else. I had also planned to record the
work for Time-Life Incorporated, and the parts showed up only just
in time. I began to ask myself: is all the quasi-innocent telephone
questioning simply a way of making off with materials? Is performance and recording (always altering a few accidentals to avoid
copyright) another kind of highway robbery? I saw the beginnings
of a vast, planned movement which would eventually harm the very
musicologists who had made everything possible. I remained silent
from that moment on.

The whole matter is succinctly summed up by a long-time member of my organization, Edgar Fleet, who gave one of the earliest
performances of the *Combattimento di Tancredi e Clorinda* using
the elaborate ornaments not found in Malipiero's edition:

> I owe countless magnificent musical experiences to you but, more than
> that, you have shown me consistently and continually, by example, how
> to approach the musical task, doing so yourself with the sincerity befitt-
> ing a true musician, and the ability based on full and adequate prepara-
> tion. Even now musicians are claiming the discovery of music which
> you showed to the world years ago. I cannot however recall a single
> occasion when you chose to claim a position of self-importance. The
> greatest thing I have learned from you is that one must serve the music
> and never make the music one's servant.

*   *   *

There are two splendid ways of spreading good news: education
and entertainment, and by coincidence these were the two pillars on
which, many years ago, BBC programs were built. In 1955 I had
begun to give recitals of the later madrigals, notably book 8, which
in 1964 we would record for Vanguard. Realizing the importance of
that "third something"—occasional music—I was pleased to find
in the *Madrigali Guerrieri ed Amorosi* several compositions
brought into being by historical events. At least one of them I borrowed for a Third Program feature by Henry Reed, *Vincenzo: a
Tragi-Comedy,* brilliantly produced by Douglas Cleverdon in 1955.
He, Henry and I worked in ideal collaboration on a radio play that,
for all its fiction, was partly based on fact, for the entire script had

7.20 MONTEVERDI
A concert of music from his
seventh and eighth books of
madrigals

Altri canti d'Amor
Canzonetta: Chiome d'oro
Con che soavità
Perchè t'en fuggi o Fillide?
Lamento della Ninfa
Ballo: Tirsi e Clori

The Deller Consort:
April Cantelo, Eileen McLoughlin
Alfred Deller
Wilfred Brown, Gerald English
Maurice Bevan

The Macgibbon String Quartet:
Margot Macgibbon, Lorraine du Val
Jean Stewart, Lilly Phillips
Robert Donington (viola da gamba)
Henry Revell (viola da gamba)
Ambrose Gauntlett (viola da gamba)
Eugene Cruft (double-bass)
Desmond Dupré (lute)
Denis Vaughan (harpsichord)
Eric Gritton (harpsichord)
Clifton Helliwell (organ)
Produced by Denis Stevens

Third Programme broadcast, early 1955

been inspired by Maria Bellonci's *A Prince of Mantua* [*I Segreti dei Gonzaga*].

My task was to supply appropriate music for this Mantuan epic. For the coronation music I drew on *Altri canti d'Amor,* and for dance music on the composer's Mantuan colleague Salomone Rossi. In search of a canzonetta I went to Monteverdi's teacher Giaches de Wert, while a notable contribution came from the opera *Arianna.* In the scene where Vincenzo is listening to the opera with his young son Silvio, we hear, beneath their quiet dialogue, the strains of the famous Lament. For this I reconstructed the lost orchestral accompaniment, and the result (to judge from a recent replay of the original broadcast) is still moving and dramatic.

Spending the years 1955–56 in America, where I held visiting

'VINCENZO'

A TRAGI-COMEDY BY HENRY REED

Produced by Douglas Cleverdon

Vincenzo Gonzaga, *Prince of Mantua*............Hugh Burden
The Duke of Mantua, *his father*................................Newton Blick
The Duchess, Leonora of Austria, *his mother*............Mary O' Farrell
Barbara Sanseverino, *Countess of Sala*........................Margaretta Scott
Ippolita Torelli...Rachel Gurney
Agnese del Caretto..Barbara Couper
Adriana Basile..Marjorie Westbury
Elena...Molly Lawson
Margherita Farnese, *Vincenzo's first wife*....................Gwen Cherrell
Ranuccio, her brother (*as a boy*)..............................Glyn Dearman
     (*as a man*)....................................Derek Hart
Carlo Borromeo..Neville Hartley
Eleonora de' Medici, *Vincenzo's second wife*.....................Barbara Lott
Francesco de' Medici, *Eleonora's father*.......................Norman Shelley
Bianca Cappello, *Francesco's second wife*......................Gladys Young
Silvio Gonzaga..D. Bryer
Gianfrancesco Sanvitale..Frank Duncan
Marcello Donati..Robert Marsden
A Florentine Mother..Cecile Chevreau

The music arranged by Denis Stevens from Mantuan composers including Frescobaldi, Gastoldi, Merulo, Monteverdi, Rossi, and de Wert

April Cantelo (*soprano*) Desmond Dupré (*lute*)
Charles Spinks (*harpsichord and organ*) The Ambrosian Singers
An Instrumental Ensemble (*led by Neville Marriner*) Directed by Denis Stevens
The time is the late Renaissance in Italy, between the years 1580 and 1612. The scenes are Mantua, Parma, Florence, Venice, and Colorno

Radio Times billing for *Vincenzo*

professorships at Cornell and Columbia, I allowed Monteverdi to be temporarily superseded by Thomas Tomkins, for the tercentenary of his death was then approaching. This period of study resulted in a book and two recordings. In the last two I enjoyed the collaboration of John de Sola Mosely, a gifted young sound engineer who even at that time was close to solving important problems having to do with stereo. We taped two programs, one of madrigals and consort music, the other of anthems and organ music. Since stereo tapes could not then be made into discs, as no system for pressing and publication existed, they were released in America as open-reel tapes and received a lengthy review by Harold Schonberg in *The New York Times*. For the first time ever, listeners could hear the "decani-cantoris" alternation from two sides of the choir.

I hoped to do the same for Monteverdi at a later stage, aiming to present his church music with comparable spatial contrast—

although it transpired that the alternation took place between two small groups of soloists in the pulpit of Nine Lessons and in the *pergola,* so accurately depicted by Canaletto in one of his rare interior illustrations. I comforted myself with the knowledge that one of the *Songs* by Tomkins "How great delight") was based on the translation of a poem by Guarini, *Con che soavità,* which was set by Monteverdi and appeared in one of our broadcasts with the Ambrosian Singers on the Third Programme in 1957.

My passionate wish was to educate the public. This I achieved to some extent by writing, broadcasting and editing. Giving an illustrated talk in the spring of 1959 on "The Interpretation of Monteverdi," I received in addition to the usual press notices a post-card from a supportive vicar in Nottinghamshire.

Collaborating with other scholars, notably Nigel Fortune and Denis Arnold, I produced concerts of songs, duets and madrigals by Monteverdi and his contemporaries in Ferrara, Venice and Modena. I sensed that interest was growing with every venture. One concert, which included the 1607 *Scherzi Musicali,* gave me a chance to show that the rhythmic subtleties of *Orfeo* could be

From: - the Reverend J. H. Blore
    the Vicarage, Shirebrook, Mansfield, Notts
1st. April 1959.

Musicologist thrice-blest - thank you for Monteverdi redivivus this evening. Quite inspiring: tho' even stripped to the bone his music has magic in it. ~ Can you persuade all performers to embrace your reading of it? ~
    Yours sincerely
        J. H. Blore

Anglican support

Message from Igor Stravinsky

found—and dealt with—in a collection of light music composed in the same year.

It was simply a case of understanding the hemiola and how to bar it for modern performance. By this time members of the Ambrosian Consort and the Deller Consort were able to sense these matters without being warned. I was therefore surprised when, many years later in 1993, I happened to review a "modern" performance of this type of music by a much-touted group with little idea of a rhythmical shift which we had already mastered a third of a century previously!

With regard to editions, I had published *Il Ballo delle Ingrate* in 1960 with the missing second violin part restored, and an English singing translation as well as Rinuccini's Italian text. In the next edition from the *Madrigali guerrieri ed amorosi* I chose the *Combattimento,* because I had come across unknown vocal ornaments in the tenor part-book. Making an English translation seemed unwise, in view of the rapid declamatory passages that dominate the episode describing the conflict. I therefore opted for a line-by-line translation at the foot of each page, so that the soloists could see exactly what they were singing about. Stravinsky, always interested in our plans, sent a note of thanks.

The time had come for a decisive step forward. In 1961 I formally registered the name "Accademia Monteverdiana" under which we would work in future as a performance and recording ensemble, which had grown out of the Ambrosian Singers in view of the need for a touring group. Consisting basically of five singers and a harpsichordist, its complement could vary almost infinitely depending on the type of concert and the locale. In Westminster Cathedral, for instance, during the Prom season of 1974, we would grow to 100 singers and players.

The immediate prospect however was the City of Bath Festival, to which we had been invited by Yehudi Menuhin, and for the inaugural concert he, with Robert Masters and Kinloch Anderson, joined the vocal quintet. Nadia Boulanger graciously agreed to attend, and the idea of a concert with my spoken introduction ap-

Rehearsal for Accademia Monteverdiana début, Bath Festival, 1961. Yehudi Menudin, Robert Masters, Kinloch Anderson, D.S. A faded inscription (top left) from Yehudi Menudin: "Ours is a happy life, dear Denis! May it long keep us together in these our high spirits! Yehudi"

peared to go down well with the critics. Most found it evocative and novel, pointing up the role of music in history and the part played by musicians in the development of new musical styles. But if education showed its hand tentatively, it was the voices and instruments that left a sonorous and lasting impression.

Years later when we gave a program featuring Monteverdi in the Lucerne Festival, Dr. Kurt von Fischer wrote what he felt about sound and words:

> Thinking of you the words come to mind: "Monteverdi" and "monti." Looking back I still remember one of our first encounters when you spent your holidays in the Swiss "monti" at "Mons Angelorum" [*Engelberg*] after having, very successfully, conducted your wonderful choir in Luzern. And there was another meeting when you came to lecture at my Institute on musical life in Venice in Monteverdi's time. It is your special gift to present music in real sound as well as by spoken and written words, to make people understand that music has to do with nature and with culture: monti and Monteverdi.

*   *   *

Culture of a Monteverdian cast set its own pace in the summer of 1961—"what a number!" as Nadia Boulanger had written in her note of acceptance. But right-side up or upside-down, the year made progress not so much with madrigals and occasional pieces, as with a full-scale work, the *Vespers of 1610,* which I had been bidden to conduct in Westminster Abbey at a concert in aid of the Historic Churches Preservation Trust. Its energetic Secretary, Hugh Llewellyn Jones, arranged for two performances to be given, and these were preceded by a recording for the BBC Transcription Service.

Novello engraved the score in record time, so that every musician had a copy of the new edition in time for the first rehearsal. Sir Adrian Boult conducted the Philomusica of London in Bach's *Overture in C major,* and the *Vespers* followed with a group of seven soloists (Heather Harper, Mary Thomas, Janet Baker, Wilfred Brown, David Galliver, John Noble and Richard Standen), the Ambrosian Singers and two organs: the Mander portable played by Dr. Roy Jesson, and the Abbey organ by Sir William McKie, who had taught me score-reading at Oxford.

Almost as soon as the concerts were announced they were over-suscribed, and hundreds had to be turned away. The Dean, in a preliminary talk with me, had predicted a large audience of nearly 2,000, but pointed out that severely limited toilet facilities would cause problems if there were an interval half-way through. Could I shorten the *Vespers?* I saw his point and decided to omit the five motets, leaving only the choral items and some plainsong antiphons I had supplied. This was not an ideal solution, but it made for a feasible evening and gave the audience a more slender, perhaps more liturgical view of the music.

On the whole, London's critics welcomed the "new look" Vespers. I would have done better to restore the missing items in a revised edition of the score as soon as possible, but this followed after a too lengthy period of 33 years. In the meanwhile listeners enjoyed "this rich music in the noble acoustic of the Abbey" (*Financial Times*) and agreed with *The Times* that the effect of the changes was "to unify what had been forced apart, and to reveal the singleness of Monteverdi's purpose beneath the apparently unfailing diversity of his stylistic means."

Based now in America for eight months of each year, I taught first of all as Distinguished Visiting Professor at Pennsylvania State University, traveling weekly by car and train to Columbia University in New York to take charge of seminars in musicology, and to help Ph.D. candidates through their dissertations. On free days I gave guest lectures, often stressing my Monteverdian connection, and continued to write and edit. Performances and recordings took place during the four summer months, when our discography steadily increased. Sir William McKie, on a visit to us in London in October 1963, wrote this note in our visitors' album: "Best wishes to you all. What a *good* education your children must be having! They will be citizens of the world." Anthony, Daphne, and Michael all helped in various ways and became well aware of Monteverdi's growing acceptance.

In the organization of the Accademia I was often assisted by my first wife Sheila, and from 1976 onwards by my second wife Lillian. Indebted not only to them, I was also constantly aware of the gratitude I felt towards friends and colleagues who, in the nature of things, frequently became my critics, more often than not in a positive sense, for they filled important posts in some of the world's finest newspapers and magazines. Themselves writers and musi-

cians, they knew something of the obstacles that had to be overcome in the preparation of a new edition, recording, or concert, and
I often felt that my task was made easier and more pleasant by this
ensemble of virtuoso writers.

Our American tour took place in 1967, including concerts in New
York, Boston, and other nearby venues. Hugues Cuénod joined us
for a performance of the Vespers in St. Paul's Chapel, Columbia
University, when Edgar Fleet (singing the echo tenor part at the
bottom of a flight of stone stairs) suddenly found himself in pitch
darkness when his candle blew out. As usual, everything flowed on
and nobody noticed anything untoward. A similar contretemps happened in Lisbon Cathedral, when Fleet sang first tenor and was
echoed by a half-hidden Leslie Fyson, a doughty ex-King's College
choral scholar. His story recalls a familiar anecdote of the off-stage
trumpeter in *Leonora No. 3,* when an officer of the law apprehends
the intending "wrong-doer." In Leslie's case his echo was nearly
cut off by an armed guard appearing in the cathedral gallery, for
since the Portuguese President and state officials were all in the
building, security had been greatly upgraded. Innocence was proved
in the nick of time.

In the purely academic field, I was awarded an honorary Doctor-
ate of Humane Letters at Fairfield University, Connecticut, as a
recognition of my services to the Monteverdian cause, making
unusually good progress in 1967 which marked the 400th anniversary of the composer's birth. At the same time I became a consul-
tant to the Time-Life Corporation, serving them also as a writer and
conductor. For an album entitled "From the Renaissance," we recorded the *Gloria* and *Hor che'l ciel e la terra,* in which I tried to
be alert to the unwritten flexibilities in tempo and observant of the
necessary *ficta* # on the third note of the long tenor solo beginning
"son lunge."

To work with the excellent Time-Life team was a genuine joy,
since everyone was extremely efficient and cooperative. The ladies
who checked copy by subdotting every word in pencil could be
counted on to save writers endless trouble. The only slight argument we had was about the true meaning of "antiphonal," but even
this was amicably resolved. One of my editors, David Johnson,
sometimes voiced the faint complaint that my pages rarely needed
much in the way of alteration. His appreciation was nevertheless
genuine, as appears from his birthday message:

David Johnson

777 DUKE STREET
ALEXANDRIA, VIRGINIA 22314
(703) 960-5000

January 11, 1982

Dear Denis:

How does one manage to attain 60 still looking
like a matinee idol, retaining the manners of
an English gentleman, the serenity of an Indian
guru, the hospitality of an Italian prince,
and the humor of a Jewish novelist?

How does one spend one's life in the service
of great 16th and 17th century musicians --
editing their music and their letters, writing
about them, conducting and recording them --
without ever turning them into museum pieces
or grist for the musicological mills? And
in the process discover, rescue, bring back
to life so much of beauty so long forgotten
or misunderstood?

How does one manage to be a specialist in
Monteverdi and still love Giuseppe Verdi, not
to mention Beethoven folksong settings and
operas by Dame Ethel Smyth? (Well, perhaps
loving Dame Ethel is going too far, but listening
to her with real zest!)

How does one do it all? Seven years from now,
when I am 60, I shall still be asking that
question, still admiring your achievements and
counting your friendship among the best of mine.

Happy birthday!

David

Letter from Time-Life

The outstanding event of 1967 was an invitation from Sir William Glock to give a concert in the Promenade season. When I attended my first Prom in 1942 I never thought that one day I would take part in them, but the passing of a quarter of a century saw significant changes. Our instructions were to appear on a special platform covering the fountain in the center of the promenade area. With a varied program of madrigals and occasional pieces—the sparkling ballet music for Ferdinand III's coronation among them—we created a precedent in bringing early music to this distinguished series inaugurated by Henry Wood in 1895, the year when my father was born. The audience, seated and standing, reacted most favorably to Monteverdi's emotional appeal, with the positive result that we were invited again for the following year.

A BBC TV program about Monteverdi set us scurrying about the palace and grounds of Eltham, while invitations to give concerts abroad came from Herbert von Karajan (whom I met when taking part in his film series "The Art of Conducting"), and Dr. Walter Strebi, founder of the Lucerne International Festival in 1938.

The afternoon following our Prom appearance saw us in Salzburg, where exactly twenty-four hours after singing in the Royal Albert Hall we gave a recital in the large hall of the Mozarteum. The quintet was joined by one of my former students, Kenneth Cooper, already a fine harpsichordist and the editor of a new edition of Monteverdi's ballet *Tirsi e Clori.* After resting and rehearsing in Engelberg, we made our way to the Lucerne Festival—not to the town itself, where no hall was available, but to the nearby village of St. Urban. Our group was further augmented by an excellent string quartet, and the complex arrangements were coaxed into action by a friendly, resourceful and multilingual musician-cum-conference organizer, Robin Marchev, with whom I am still happily in touch. Also present at St. Urban were the eminent Swiss soprano Maria Stader and Dr. Pierre Tagmann, whose Mantuan researches have since proved invaluable.

*   *   *

Increasingly surrounded by Monteverdiana, I began to be concerned about the state of his correspondence. Realizing the enormous importance of his thoughts about music and its performance, I asked Dr. Nino Pirrotta whether he felt that the letters could ever be translated satisfactorily. Various extracts had been translated from time to time, and a few letters appeared in anthologies. But the only Italian edition was unreliable, and Pirrotta said that many passages were almost meaningless to him—born Italian with a penchant for solving problems—and must be even more difficult for foreigners. Since misleading translations had been based on a corrupt Italian text, it took time to put things right. At this point I jumped in, confident that I could complete the task in five years. It actually took fifteen. Although many kind friends helped me, I wonder whether they thought me at times a little unhinged.

I was living in Santa Barbara when serious work began, and the spacious house I purchased (after a firm university appointment had been made) contained all the books and music required. But by a dastardly act of deceit and dishonesty, the appointment was abolished, probably due to the evil work of a cur rather than a man. I then remembered that Monteverdi had been robbed at gun-point on his way from Mantua to Venice, and remembered that he too sensed a plot, the robbers and coach-driver all party to it.

Three-and-a-half centuries later, I found myself in a similar position. Suddenly without teaching duties, I threw myself into research and translation, completing the book by 1979. In the course of my work, frequent repetitions of phrases and sentiments took me in their grip, so that after a short time I began to feel the way the composer must have felt about some of the potentially disastrous hurdles that life can throw in one's way.

Remote from Europe, I was however able to visit once a year, carrying on with recordings and performances when opportunity offered. These included conducting in S. Marco, appearances at festivals, and exploration of the music of Monteverdi's contemporaries—Schütz, Luzzaschi, Gesualdo, Nenna—and of his immediate predecessors such as Gastoldi, De Wert, Vicentino and the Gabrielis. I now found that my efforts were approved not only by early-music experts, but by modernists like Jonathan Cott and Robert Craft. In a *New York Sunday Times* article, "The Avant-Garde of the Renaissance," Cott stated that

> the musicologist and conductor DS has single-handedly been introducing us to the music of Willaert, De Wert, Andrea Gabrieli, and now Pomponio Nenna. His recordings with the London-based Ambrosian Singers and Accademia Monteverdiana are essential material for devotees of Renaissance music.

Choral-instrument concert in S. Marco, Venice, August 1972

Yet it was not so single-handed after all, for I enjoyed the active cooperation and interest of Henry Kaufmann, Carol MacClintock, Gustave Reese and Glenn Watkins, to name but a few. In the New York world, Craft felt that

> the most completely successful is Vanguard's "Music from the Court of Mantua: Giaches de Wert." Wert is a great composer. On a night when a lid of foul air is clamped over the city's noise-besotted streets, one of these songs by De Wert is guaranteed to bring relief. The forms are minuscule, but not the emotion, which retains a freshness that some more recent and more 'searing' passions have lost.

After many years of happy collaboration with Gregg International Press (its far-seeing president Newton Gregg, with his wife Lucile, had been strong supporters over the years), I suggested a facsimile reprint of the 1615 edition of *Orfeo*. Questions I had often pondered about the advanced harmonies of this opera were raised in a letter from Roland Jackson.

*   *   *

Of all our Trustees, Yehudi Menuhin was certainly one of the most encouraging and receptive, for he invited us several times to the Bath Festival, London, Windsor, and last but not least to Gstaad, where I believe we gave some of our most inspired performances. It was an unalloyed pleasure to prepare and give concerts in the lovely old church at Saanen, with its frescoes dating from two centuries before Monteverdi's time. As at the Bath Festival many years before, we enjoyed the cooperation of Yehudi and his colleagues and the spirited company of his wife Diana.

Distractions and amusements included the appearance of the Monteverdi car, built by a Swiss firm directed (it was said) by one of the composer's descendants. Seated in the luxurious vehicle at an exhibition one day, I felt immediately comfortable but realized it was quite out of the ordinary—like Claudio's music.

By the early seventies many other Monteverdi groups, choirs and organizations had sprung into existence, and it was not difficult to perceive that they relied heavily on the repertoire we had uncovered in previous years. I like to think that imitation can sometimes be a form of flattery, but the main point was that "the message" had started to circulate.

When Faber & Faber published the *Letters* in 1980, reviews ap-

CLAREMONT GRADUATE SCHOOL

CLAREMONT, CALIFORNIA 91711

Dear Denis:

At 60 you can look back, as could Monteverdi, on many splendid accomplishments. And may you enjoy, as he did, many more fruitful years. But whatever more you do, we appreciate the things you have already given us, your sensitive performances, your wise writings, your personal helpfulness. May this be a time of new beginnings, of discoveries, of bringing together past insights, of courage for the difficult, of pleasure in all that is lovely and rewarding.

As admirers of Monteverdi's art we have often admired, and yet been puzzled by certain of his dissonances. So strange to the ear are they, and yet so right, so convincing. How were these peculiar formations conceived by an ear nurtured on Renaissance polyphony? Here are some recent thoughts I have had that I will throw out as speculations.

Could this be a substitute preparation? In place of a more normal g, creating a lower neighboring note on f#, could Monteverdi have substituted another note from the same g chord, a b♭, creating a bold appoggiatura?

Could this be a substitute resolution? Instead of passing normally to e, the d proceeds to another note in the E chord, a g#. The note d, rather than being a passing tone becomes an escape tone.

Could this be a "chordal" suspension? The solo voice was given the power to pull an entire chord to its resolution. This simply extends the earlier 2-3 suspension.

Denis, our best to you on this day. May the many letters you receive testify to the affection we all have for you.

Roland Jackson

THE CLAREMONT COLLEGES ■ ■ ■ ■ ■
Claremont Graduate School / Pomona College / Scripps College / Claremont Men's College / Harvey Mudd College / Pitzer College

Letter from Roland Jackson

Gstaad Festival, August 17, 1974. John Noble, Nigel Rogers, Edgar Fleet, Yehudi Menudin, Patricia Clark, Ursula Connors, Shirley Minty

peared in many cities, welcoming a ray of light in an obscure corner of musical history. A valued personal tribute came from Nino Pirrotta, who produced a brilliant parody of an "unknown" letter and then followed it with an equally pointed parody of my translation style. The letter begins:

Molto Ill.re Sig.re et pad.n Osser.mo

Sto solecitando l'aurum purissimo da un tal Sig.r Medico de' Santi di pelo rosso qual si diletta molto di investigare la pietra filosofica. . . .

My Very Illustrious Lord and Most Esteemed Master

I keep asking a certain Signor Doctor de Santi, with red hair, who greatly enjoys investigating the philosopher's stone, for the purest gold. If he is not the one, I know of no other who can teach me anything as valuable as Your Lordship's merits to make a present with on the occasion of Your sixtieth birthday. For which reason Your Lordship will have me excused if I shall be only able, on such most propitious day, to offer the wishes of all my heart that Your many and many days be always as happy. I regret with all my soul being unable to be there to join the Chorus of all Your admirers and relatives; all the same, making reverence to my Very Illustrious Lord Signor Dionigi Stefaneschi with all affection, I pray God for the peak of your every perfect happiness, sending You news as to how I am at present engaged in making fire under a glass beaker (see the Book of my letters, pp. 291 and 303) with some written words of you on its top, to extract something from them, and make something of it, so that (please God) I may then cheerfully explain this something to My Lord Stefaneschi. From Rome, 16 January 1982

Your Very Illustrious Lordship's
ever most grateful servant
Claudio Monteverdi

(through the hand of N. P., translated with the help of D. S.)

Another friend who recalled the role of the *Letters* within a general discussion of editing and musical performance was Dr. Warren Kirkendale, in his Latin letter, sent on my 60th anniversary, recalling the Bellagio Congress.

VARRENUS DIONYSIO S.P.D.

APTISSIMUM EST, STUDIOSUM, QUI RECENTER EDITIONEM EXEMPLAREM EPISTULARUM IN LUCEM DEDERIT, HONORARE LITTERIS CONLEGARUM IN OCCASIONE DIEI NATALIS SEXAGESIMI . . .

Warren bids a very hearty greeting to Denis. It is very appropriate, on his sixtieth birthday, to honour with letters from his colleagues a scholar who has recently published an exemplary edition of letters. May my epistle, filled with happy memory, assent to the general list of your serious accomplishments by which, with great authority, you have brought back to new life many of the best musical works of the past in editions and records. In the summer of 1974 a small number of your friends took part with great joy not only in the recreation of such works but also in their ambience. For hardly were we guests in the royal Italian house of the sixteenth century in those memorable days at the Villa Serbelloni, than you brought from London angelic voices for the performance of madrigals that we prepared in handwritten editions. May your life continue for many years with such harmony.

Life did indeed continue with harmony, albeit spiced with a touch of dissonance here and there, together with an enforced reassessment of certain public contact areas. In the 1980s, the publishing of music and musicography suffered massive setbacks, and I assume that the few winners in this economic changeover were those photocopying corporations that have effectively removed much of the world's copyright protection. A lawyer-composer friend, visiting China recently to discuss copyright procedure as it might affect this nation of well over one billion citizens, had an interview with a leading authority in Beijing. "What is copylight?" asked his interlocutor.

The first edition of the *Letters* elicited more than two dozen reviews and found a welcoming public, but when the revised and enlarged edition came out fifteen years later it proved to be a very different story. This was equally true of music, records and copyrights. Although the Accademia had by this time achieved its principal object, it could not expect the kind of sponsorship that underpinned more recent productions. We were able to take a few curtain calls, notably at our final Promenade concert when a Venetian program led listeners from the era of motets celebrating fifteenth-century doges as far as the Monteverdi *Gloria,* and at the concerts in London and Washington DC where the viability of other Vespers than the 1610 collection stirred conductors to renew their activity and experimentation.

I had long before taken up Monsignor Giuseppe Biella's suggestion that the composer, who claimed to write a new set of Vespers every Christmas and possibly at other times, was in fact reusing his many psalm settings to fit the various liturgies that flowed past him throughout the year. I had introduced the concept of a *Christmas Vespers* first at the Proms (1969), then at a special concert at St. John's, Smith Square, to coincide with a recording commissioned by Midland Bank International. This concert was repeated in a vast ecclesiastical edifice in Washington, DC, the National Shrine of the

Immaculate Conception, where I had the fulfilling experience of conducting the work in its liturgical context with a priest as celebrant.

In her *Washington Post* account of the concert, Joan Reinthaler rightly drew attention to the preparatory work of the choir director.

The author at Christmas Vespers, Washington, DC, 1979

The choir sang with unfailing beauty and a thorough understanding of the difficult stylistic touches that characterize all of Monteverdi's music. This ease and familiarity with the idiom is Stevens' work . . . but the remarkable vocal accuracy, absolute pitch perfection and choral balance are a testimony to the training and leadership of choir-master Robert Shafer.

Although a review such as this indicated the influence of our Accademia publications on the world, and on large groups performing in spacious buildings, comments on a more intimate kind of recital proved that other styles and idioms could also offer a challenge. At Gstaad our work continued, and we were able to give an overview of eight centuries of church music or a survey of seven centuries of Petrarch settings. On another evening we offered a panorama of secular music by composers from four nations. A review from *Les Feuilles d'Avis de Lausanne* summed up the general impression:

> Admirable Accademia! In their concert I saw a kind of central coronation of the Gstaad Festival—from Goudimel to Monteverdi, from Lassus to Purcell, to Haydn as well. The five singers succeeded in a prodigious demonstration of high-strung mannerism, enhanced by the excellence of those accompanying.

Cooperation with musicians is one of the most important essentials in a successful concert or tour. I have no time for displays of temper or attempts to make artists feel small—indeed for the purpose of performance I am happier when they feel larger than life. But if soloists and instrumentalists are of immense importance, continuo players are so, too, for they supply the ever-needed harmonic support for vast areas of early music. I have worked happily with many fine continuo players, among whom Leslie Pearson always proved himself an outstanding artist:

> As a keyboard continuo player it is always a delight to work with you because you have the rare ability of allowing the performer the freedom of self-expression, and yet still maintaining an overall firm but gentle control which is the result of your experience, intelligence, scholarship and innate sense of style.

*   *   *

One aspect of music-making is the continuation of old friendships, and on returning to England I once again found friends and colleagues who had temporarily lost touch. I have made new friends, too, and respect their new views on old music. If I see them less frequently than before, it is because I am busy with the future, especially as it concerns misunderstood matters of scholarship or the improvement of my own work. If somehow I manage to bring out revised versions of books, scores and records, I relish the luxury of correcting my own misprints; so that I am still working for those who may one day need guidance.

I am glad that my dissertation-supervising eye has not yet failed, for it serves me in good stead when I drop in at the odd concert or listen in to a still odder radio. My experience on the air taught me that different shades of opinion should be heard if we are not to descend into militant fascism. But there is now no sharing of air-time. Five or six "names" ring the changes on themselves, regurgitating the same borrowed platitudes, the same puerile prejudices.

The reason for this is not hard to find. Youth wishes to assert itself, and the only way it knows is to tear down the achievement of past masters. Did I do the same? I think not, for I had no wish to demolish my elders and betters—provided they had proved reliable. I wanted to turn to them again and again, building on the legacy they left behind.

Just as I could read a graduate student's essay and tell the sources he had used, so nowadays I find it a simpler matter to know where this or that radio commentator found his purple plums. The same is true of musical journalism, which is almost totally transparent and pathetically reminiscent of Grove's Dictionary. The sorrowful lack of accurate steering on Radio Three prompted me to write to *The Daily Telegraph* in November 1993 about the Monteverdi broadcasts:

> Radio Three, in its infinite wisdom, has turned what should have been a commemoration of Monteverdi's death into what it calls "a celebration."
>
> Unfortunately it has cheapened the event with a surfeit of performances which failed to present the composer's work as he intended. Instead of following the most up-to-date editions of his music, Radio Three has used 60-year-old editions which are inaccurate and employ what we know to be false harmonies and texts.
>
> As a result, the performances totally lacked inspiration.
>
> This could have been acceptable if the BBC had not produced an excellent performance of *Orfeo* in 1952 when Walter Goehr conducted an epoch-making performance in Studio 1, Maida Vale.

As producer of that broadcast, I accomplished two important tasks. One was to approve the amended orchestration of the last three acts, in which the composer's efforts had diminished because of the great pressures under which he was working.

The other was to reveal hidden metrical implications, at that time unsuspected, by re-barring much of the score, which was tacitly followed in all subsequent editions.

There was a nine-person continuo section, all using reproductions of early instruments. The vocal artists included Pierre Bernac, Irma Kolassi, Alfred Deller and Wilfred Brown.

I recently returned from America after an absence of 20 years, and therefore think I know just how horrified Monteverdi would feel were he to be awake today.

Any summing-up of a situation must set positive aspects against the negative ones. If a scholar-musician proves several times over that the right continuo instrument for concertos by Vivaldi and his contemporaries is the organ, the necessary adjustment will not happen straight away. After all, it ranks as a frightfully demanding concept, as readers of my *Early Music* book will realize. The adjustment may take decades. Similarly if one finds that Martinelli is still being mistaken for Monteverdi, or that a hemiola continues to be misread, the solution will surely fall into place in the fullness of time. The general public, aware of so many things, is slow to take in the obvious where music is concerned.

My last years have been given up to twin tasks. One was a translation of all the songs and poems Monteverdi set to music, a small volume published in 1998 by Long Barn Books. Perhaps these translations will provoke less eyestrain than the tiny print of the average CD booklet.

The other task is a complete edition of the composer's final masterpiece, his *Selva morale e spirituale* of 1640, due to form part of the new Monteverdi *Opera Omnia* issued by the Fondazione Claudio Monteverdi in Cremona. In years to come, those massive volumes may shed some light on the musicianship that informs Monteverdi's prose and the logical process of his musical thought.

2

"I, Claudio Monteverdi"

FOR ONCE BOLDLY PUTTING *himself forward (not one of his letters begins in this way), Monteverdi addressed his immediate superiors at S. Marco and recounted, in a resounding display of rhetoric, the events that took place outside the basilica on June 8, 1637. So powerful and sustained is the flow of his thought that he delays the main verb until the last third of the letter. Its text has often been reprinted, and the various editors and translators are listed on p. 429 of* The Letters of Claudio Monteverdi *(revised edition, Clarendon Press, 1995). You will find the uncensored text of the letter on p. 431.*

With evident distaste, the composer quotes the Venetian gutter-language in which Aldegati chose to express himself, and in due course this troublesome singer was censured by the authorities and dropped from the choir.

By the time this scandal took place the bulk of the *Selva morale* had been assembled and was already stacked up in Bartolomeo Magni's printing shop. The part-books would appear in less than three years. The complete compilation would see the light in 1641, re-emerge three centuries later in Malipiero's edition, and once again in a modern edition by the Fondazione Claudio Monteverdi in 1999.

I discussed the background of this work in 1967 at a Monteverdi congress in Cremona. All the congress papers were edited by Raffaello Monterosso and published as *Claudio Monteverdi e il suo tempo* at Verona in 1969.

Returning now to the same topic, I realize the inadequacies of that juvenile contribution, but rejoice to know that the passing of years has provided me with new viewpoints, many of them opened up by colleagues working in similar fields.

While in Cremona I purchased a small book by Elia Santoro, *Ico-*

nografia Monteverdiana, one page of which shows just how slowly scholarly information disseminates. The last of a series of photographic illustrations reproduces an old painting, then little known and now lost, that portrays the composer aged 43 or 44. Seated next to him is the Neapolitan *diva* Adriana Basile, who has Monteverdi's son Francesco on her right and next to him her husband. Although brought to light all those years ago, it was not re-discovered until 1994.

On the other hand, a false portrait of the composer—actually of the Mantuan actor Tristano Martinelli—has appeared in at least ten different publications, yet was shown to be the wrong one as long ago as 1978.[1] Unfortunately this error cannot be eradicated; and the same may also become true of errors surrounding the *Selva.*

I mention this portrait because it was painted in Mantua about 1611 or 1612, years that form a watershed between two of his most important publications—the *Sacrae Cantiunculae* of 1582 and the *Selva morale e spirituale* of 1641. They were the alpha and omega of the compositions issued during his own lifetime.

Both were devoted to church music.

ORIGINS OF THE *SELVA*

Orazio Vecchi gives us one of the clearest definitions of this term in his *Selva di varia recreatione:*

> so as not to follow a continuous line, just as we find trees placed in woods without that order one is used to seeing in artificial gardens.[2]

Monteverdi's *Selva,* in two sections, might seem to divide neatly into "morale" (part A) and "spirituale" (part B). Although in the individual books both parts have separate paginations, part A in the *tavola* has no page references whereas part B does. In addition, the letter "B" is placed too high, as if it refers to *Ab aeterno ordinata sum.* It should be a new heading for the sequence of psalms beginning *Dixit Dominus.*

As it happens, Monteverdi's *Selva* is of the Vecchi type, for the compositions are to some extent mixed, moral and spiritual items

---

1. Pamela Askew, "Fetti's 'Portrait of an Actor' Reconsidered," *The Burlington Magazine* 120 (1978): 59.
2. Venezia, Gardano, 1590.

being intermingled. For example, the first five works are moral, while those following count as spiritual. At the very end comes the *Pianto della Madonna,* another "moral" work in which Arianna's Lament is transformed after the manner of Aquilino Coppini's *Musica tolta* of 1607 into a moving search for the divine.

The origins of this remarkable collection are usually associated with the latter part of Monteverdi's career, perhaps from the time of the ceremonies for the end of the plague in 1631 or the composer's becoming a priest in 1632. A careful man, he liked to keep his compositions for many years until his shelf almost reached breaking point. The result of this habit can be seen in the *Mass and Vespers* (1610) which took him fifteen years, or the *Sesto libro de madrigali* (1614) which needed at least eight years. Although he wrote several shorter works for anthologies printed between 1615 and 1629, he held back the psalm, hymn, and Magnificat settings, perhaps because he thought there would be less demand for them.

His arrival in Venice in 1613 launched a period of intense creative activity. For once in his life he was well housed, well paid, and sufficiently pressured to ensure a constant stream of works for private and public consumption. Those thirty years witnessed the production of church music for S. Marco and its festivals, liturgical and para-liturgical; it also saw the genesis of minor masterpieces such as the five pieces with Italian texts that open the *Selva.* These were first performed at informal Sunday afternoon gatherings at the great palaces of Girolamo Mocenigo, Sigismund III of Poland or his son Prince Ladislao, the Duke of Neuburg, Sir Isaac Wake, or Giovanni Matteo Bembo. Music-loving hosts in Venice were usually in a position to offer the most lavish hospitality, and none of them failed to invite the Maestro di cappella.[3]

Works destined for the *Selva* could have originated as early as 1614, leaving more than twenty years until 1638, the cut-off date for publication. Two last-minute contributions, printed at the end of the books, survive from a small but colorful ceremony held on May 17, 1637. This was the translation of the body of S. Giovanni Martire, duca d'Alessandria, to a new sepulchre in the middle of the nunnery church of S. Daniele near the Arsenal.[4]

---

3. See Claudio Monteverdi, *Lettere,* a cura di Éva Lax (Olschki: Firenze, 1994); *The Letters of Claudio Monteverdi,* translated and edited by Denis Stevens (Oxford: The Clarendon Press, 1995).

4. Sansovino, *Venetia città nobilissima* (Venezia: Curti, 1663), 23.

The motet *Jubilet tota civitas* is scored for soprano voices designated only by "Canta" and "Tacet." Although its text suggests a
male saint and martyr, the high tessitura indicates female range—
which turns out to be partly true. The three notes originally marked
"N" probably stood for the three syllables "Jo-han-nes," and the
alternating soprano parts could have been intended for the leading
castrato of S. Marco and the nuns of S. Daniele.

Another jubilant motet used at the same ceremony was *Laudate
Dominum in sanctis ejus* (Psalm 150), written for a virtuoso tenor
and organ continuo, which makes generous use of the chaconne
theme of *Zefiro torna*.[5] Monteverdi's letter of June 9, 1637, to the
Procurators tells of a violent quarrel over the fees for this engage-
ment outside the door of S. Marco on June 8th.

The origins of the *Selva* go back even further than 1614. When
the Thanksgiving Mass was performed on November 21, 1631, a
state of enormous excitement prevailed. Something had to go
wrong, and what happened was that since the musical forces required two basic positions in the basilica and two extra *palchi,* four
sets of music had to be prepared for two small groups and double
choir who as usual occupied the *pergola* and other sections of the
edifice. After the service, with fireworks, cannon and liquid refresh-
ments, the person deputed to return the music to Monteverdi was
robbed, probably by one of the composer's enemies. It was never
recovered.[6]

The composer was of course furious, since nobody had made a
safety copy. As he had no intention of writing out the missing parts
of the *Credo,* one of Magni's assistants may have suggested using
a Mass already submitted, and "troping" it with the surviving *concertato* items. We realize today that they do not fit as regards key,
and even less well stylistically, since the time-gap between the four-
part Mass and the *Credo* was about forty-three years.

The Mass, written in Cremona shortly after 1587, is based on the
opening theme of the madrigal *La vaga pastorella* from the *Primo
Libro de madrigali.* Since at that time, it was still permissible to
write a parody Mass based on a madrigal Monteverdi did so, without even so much as a blush. Perhaps he wished to justify the inclu-
sion of such an early work in a supposedly late collection in order
to summarize, as it were, his entire musical career in one publica-

---

5. *Scherzi musicali . . .* (Venezia: Magni, 1632).
6. G. Ridolfi, *Le meraviglie di Venezia* (Venezia: Curti, 1642).

Canaletto drawing of S. Marco during Vespers, 1766

tion, which may also contain at least one work dating from the Mantuan years.

Cremona, Mantua, Venice: all reunited under one title.

The Mass is not only written in *stile antico,* it contains a strange series of cadences, the nature of which emerges when the notation is quartered to reveal a macrocosm viewpoint. The most likely explanation may be bound up with a desire to repeat certain final syllables.

THE *SELVA* AS AUTOBIOGRAPHY

Monteverdi left no autobiography. He had not the slightest idea that many centuries after his death his music and letters would be unceasingly published and republished. Even if nothing else had survived, the *Selva* would serve to summarize his life and philosophy. In old age (he was 73 when the volumes were due to be published) he took life easily and was even prepared to see publication delayed for six months, since Bartolomeo Magni's in-house proof reader had discovered a huge number of misprints. When the composer heard about them he immediately insisted on having corrections made, for the music was intended as a gift to the Empress Eleonora Gonzaga, his most important patroness. To offer her an imperfect work would be unthinkable.

Only when all was in order did he compose the dedication, dating it May 1, 1641—several months later than the printing of the title page which had already been completed with the original date of 1640. This dedication deserves to be included in any collection of his letters, since it contains at least one piece of biographical information: that he served Duke Vincenzo I (1562–1612) for twenty-two years.

Sacred and Imperial Majesty,

Having begun to consecrate my reverent service to the glories of the Most Serene House of GONZAGA when the Most Serene Lord Duke VINCENZO, Your Sacred MAJESTY's father (of happy memory), took pleasure in receiving the results of my observance, which in my green youth I tried for the space of 22 continuous years, with all diligence and with my musical talent, to show to him as being affectionate (since the interposition of the world and of time have never been able to obscure even a minuscule mark of my respect), so that the honours received either from your Most Serene Predecessors or from Your Majesty can never be afflicted by oblivion, but rather have I been, on occasion, courteously revived by them until this my mature age.

Wherefore I have been so bold as to publish this *Selva Morale e Spirituale,* dedicating it to Your Majesty, so that bearing your Sacred Name on the frontispiece, it will surely continue to show the world on every hand my grateful devotion. For this reason, in all possible humility, I beg Your Majesty to condescend to receive it, although it may not perhaps be in the state of perfection that I would wish it; but it will be a small testimony of the reverent affection which humbly and promptly I dedicate and consecrate to Your Majesty, praying for you from God the height of all peaceful prosperity. At Venice the first of May 1641.

Of Your Sacred Imperial Majesty
a most humble and most grateful servant
Claudio Monteverde

His first message to the musician-reader is a pair of compositions inspired by Petrarch, whose verses he had first set to music in two madrigals written in 1607: *Zefiro torna* and *Ohimé il bel viso*.

I straightway began setting the sonnet to music, and was engaged in doing this for six days, then two more what with trying it out and rewriting it. I worked with the same devotion of mind that I have always had in regard to every other composition written by me in order the more to serve His Highness's most delicate taste.[7]

In his *Libro Ottavo* he returns to Petrarch with *Hor che'l ciel* and *Vago augelletto*. Now in the *Selva* he salutes Petrarch for the last time and sets the opening sonnet of the *Rime sparse:*

> You who listen in scattered verse to the sound
> of those sighs with which I nourished my heart
> in my first youthful error,
> when I was in part another man from what I am;
>
> to the different ways in which I weep and reason,
> between vain hopes and vain sorrows
> where as one who understands love as a trial
> I hope to find pity and forgiveness.
>
> But I see now how to all people
> I was for a long time a legend, whence often
> I am ashamed of myself;
>
> and of my raving the fruit is shame,
> and repentance and the clear knowledge
> that what pleases on earth is a short dream.

---

7. Letter no. 4, 28 July 1607.

If read in the light of his music and his letters, this poem expresses nothing that would seem alien to the composer. He was indeed acquainted with "sighs, youthful errors, different ways, vain hopes, shame, and a short dream."

The other Petrarch text proves to be an extract from *Il Trionfo della Morte*,[8] the order of the verses rearranged in such a way that Monteverdi's hand can be perceived.

> O ye blind, of what use is it, all this toil?   88–100
> All things return to the great and ancient mother,
> and your name can hardly be found at all.
> > O ye blind!
> > Is there just one useful task then among the thousand
> that are not all out-and-out vanities?
> Whoever understands your studies, let him say Yes.
> > What use is it to conquer so many countries
> and make foreign nations tributaries
> with men, to their harm, always inflamed?
> > What use is it?
> > After vain and perilous undertakings,
> acquiring lands and treasures with blood,
> it is gentler to find for oneself water, bread,
> > glass and wood rather than gems and gold.
> > O ye blind!

> Where are the riches? where are the honours?   82–85
> > O ye blind!
> And the jewels and the sceptres and the crowns?
> > O ye blind!
> and mitres with crimson colours?
> > Wretched is the man who puts his trust in mortal matter.

As a youth he had been with Vincenzo's army in Hungary, and in his later years had learned of the destruction brought by Aldringhen's troops to Mantua. Petrarch's lines pre-echo Monteverdi's thoughts on the subjugation of people and the gathering of riches, but all this was carried out by the military missionaries of the Holy Roman Empire, partly presided over by her to whom the music was dedicated. Wretched indeed is the person who trusts in earthly goods!

He could not say that to the Empress, but Petrarch could. Relent-

---

8. Text from the *Selva morale e spirituale*.

lessly he brings back the refrain "O ciechi": you blind fools, do you not realize the error of your ways?

Associated at various times with many outstanding poets of his age, Monteverdi enjoyed the personal friendship of a chosen few. One of these in particular became an extremely enthusiastic admirer of the music to which his verses were occasionally linked— Don Abbate Angelo Grillo, writer of religious poems under his own name, and of madrigal texts as Livio Celiano.

The close relationship between Grillo and Monteverdi is revealed by their correspondence, which began about 1610 and continued intermittently until the poet's death in 1629. He first mentions a sacred madrigal of his in a letter to Monteverdi written about 1611:

> how well does your divine music correspond to the divine subject of my sacred madrigal, and how wholly celestial it becomes in your celestial harmony![9]

Two or three years later, when Monteverdi had moved to Venice, Grillo wrote again, this time from S. Nicolò del Lido, where an abundant spring of the purest water rose, and excused himself from attending the musical evenings at Giovanni Matteo Bembo's palazzo, whither organs were often carried to ensure proper music-making.

In 1614, having received one of the first copies of *Il sesto libro de madrigali*, he thanked Monteverdi, praising his music to the skies, and insisted on the importance of a few enclosed sheets of manuscript music:

> I say the same of the manuscript compositions, in which you show yourself to be so much the greater master as the help of the words is less.[10]

The explanation is clear. Madrigals always found a ready market, whereas works with a moral text often had to remain in manuscript. Grillo was nevertheless only too happy to receive them, especially if the music was as good as *È questa vita un lampo*.

Since *Il sesto libro* was a memorial volume, without a dedication but clearly in memory of the composer's wife and the young Caterina Martinelli, it is possible that this five-part composition should be considered as part of the earlier tribute:

---

9. Angelo Grillo, *Dalle lettere* (Venezia: Deuchino, 1616), 2:137.
10. Ibid., 3:128.

> This life is a flash of lightning
> which vanishes as it appears
> in this mortal field.
> For if I look at the past
> it is already dead; the future not yet born,
> and the present vanished,
> also not quite in view.
> Ah, fugitive flash, even if you please me,
> it's after the flash that the thunderbolt comes.

This poem, printed in Grillo's *Pietosi affetti*,[11] speaks of the transitory nature of human life and the fatal bolt that closes even a pleasurable existence. If not a memorial to Claudia and Caterina, it may have been set to music in 1629, shortly after Grillo died, as a personal farewell from Monteverdi. Although unsuitable for casual publication, it would certainly be apt for a volume such as the *Selva*.

Spuntava il dì renews earlier contacts with Rome, for these verses are by Francesco Balducci, one of a circle of poets surrounding Domenico Mazzocchi and the Aldobrandini family. Since the poem did not see publication until some years after the *Selva* had been issued, it must have reached Monteverdi in manuscript form. As with several of his other works, he altered the text to make it topical, even as regards rivers, so that "Tebro" becomes "Arno":

> Trees desire her,
> breezes caress her,
> the fairest flowers bow before her
> and young grasses embellish her.
> Neither Po nor Arno ever watered so lovely a flower.
>
> But what's the use?
> What could ever shield her from heaven's wrath?
> A lovely thing on earth dies and lasts not.
>
> > *La Rosa* (Francesco Balducci)

The last of the five Italian pieces is a *canzon morale* for voices and strings: *Chi vuol che m'innamori*. Its verses, alternating the sad and the cheerful, recall some of the poems in book 7, or perhaps in book 9, whose only known authors are Rinuccini and Strozzi. Its

---

11. Venezia: Giunto e Ciotti, 1608.

restricted musical resources would ensure a place in any intimate musical gathering, notably those of Ladislao, Prince of Poland, who did not like music that went on for too long.

The remaining spiritual works begin with the Missa *La vaga pastorella* and continue until *Laudate Dominum* (Ps. 150). *Il Pianto della Madonna,* the final moral contribution, serves as a pious peroration, allowing the composer to step back, survey his design, and possibly murmur *Exegi monumentum aere perennius;* for the *Selva* has indeed endured even though a mere handful of copies has been preserved, and not all of them complete. He knew perfectly well that if the selection made for Eleonora represented some of his finest music, there were many more manuscripts that could be published to increase his renown. Thanks to a minor miracle of rearrangement, he had been able to keep not only S. Marco but several other Venetian churches well supplied with his own creations for some thirty years.

This rearrangement consisted of ringing the changes on a limited number of works for use at Mass and Vespers. In the *Selva* we find:

    7 choral psalms
    4 hymns (suitable for a dozen or more texts)
    3 settings of *Salve Regina*
    2 settings of *Magnificat*
    2 Masses (one slightly dilapidated)
    2 motets
    1 psalm-motet for solo voice

Although his letters written from 1615 onwards frequently refer to his duty to compose music for the basilica, they rarely mention titles or resources, which makes it difficult to associate individual items with fixed periods in his career. A few dates can nevertheless be hazarded. Another Mass and a dozen psalms saw the light only in 1650, and these (together with a handful of other posthumous publications) could have added to his stockpile of interchangeables. On the whole they seem to have served his purpose well.

The concertante *Gloria* and fragmentary *Credo,* together with a magnificent bass aria *Ab aeterno ordinata sum* were first performed at the ceremonies on November 21, 1631, as part of a general thanksgiving for the cessation of the plague. Extra singers and instrumentalists were hired for the occasion, which Marco Ginammi, a Venetian man of letters, described in a pamphlet addressed to the city's official Resident in Naples:

> A most solemn mass was sung, composed by Mr. Claudio Monteverdi, director of music and glory of our century. In the Gloria and Credo he combined the voices with the trombones, with exquisite and marvelous harmony.[12]

The loud *trombe squarciate* were sometimes called *tromboni,* as at Mantua in 1592 when the young Monteverdi had just joined the establishment as a string player. He might have noticed, in the Third Intermezzo for Guarini's *Il pastor fido,* that the actor representing Austro, the south wind, had "in mano trombone di quelli che chiamano *squarciati.*"[13]

Within the orbit of such remarkable celebrations a concertato Mass ranked as only one out of many musical events. Another was the solemn singing of vespers, in which instrumentalists undoubtedly played a considerable role. The seven psalms contain in fact different settings that go beyond the accepted bounds in spreading an atmosphere of unusual happiness and rejoicing. These are *Dixit Dominus 1, Confitebor 3, Beatus vir 1, Laudate pueri 1* and *Laudate Dominum 1.* All five project a bright and triumphant mood, with violins, optional trombones and organ adding the necessary atmosphere of solemnity.

The first psalm, *Dixit,* appears in a more complete form here than in the 1650 collection, while the second, *Confitebor,* seems to anticipate the two madrigals published in the *Libro Ottavo: Dolcissimo uscignolo* and *Chi vol haver felice.* These two settings had almost certainly come into existence by 1623, when Monteverdi was in touch with Prince Alfonso II d'Este's Venetian agent, Dr. Alberto Colombo. Eventually the two completed madrigals went off to Ferrara, and on March 24, 1623, the Prince sent Monteverdi a letter of thanks:

> The madrigal which your honor sent me has mightily pleased everyone who heard it, and it more than made up for that slight lateness which has caused you some trouble, what with the lightness and elegance of the composition. . . . I shall be expecting you to double my pleasure and

12. The correct attribution to Marco Ginammi was first made by James H. Moore in *Venezia favorita da Maria . . . ,* 314–17.
13. Ferrara, Biblioteca comunale, MS 156, i, 27.

indebtedness with the other madrigal, and trust you can also assure me of being in good health."[14]

These late madrigals, two Guarini settings in the *Libro Ottavo,* were undoubtedly the last that Monteverdi would publish. In the meantime they could serve admirably as a double contrafactum in *Confitebor tibi Domine,* which begins with an adaptation of the second madrigal leading into an equally effective transformation of the first.

Chiome d'oro, a cheerful canzonetta that made its début in print in 1619 *(Libro Settimo),* had made many Venetian friends in the first few years of Monteverdi's residence. Free at last from troubled Mantua, whose evil men had not hesitated to send thugs to rob him at pistol-point on the way to Venice, the composer could indulge in a new freedom reflected by musical joie de vivre. It must have seemed only logical to transform *Beatus vir* into an appealing contrafactum appropriate for a time of rejoicing. Even the psalm text is pressed into service as a repetitive rondo, since the opening words *Beautus vir* return seven times, reminding us that the man who fears the Lord is blessed sevenfold. This delightful new garb for an established favorite could have smiled its way into the repertoire of S. Marco at any point after 1620, even though it had to wait two decades for its first appearance in print.

Two of the remaining psalms for vespers, *Laudate pueri* 1 and *Laudate Dominum* 1, feature instrumental support and would thus be fitting for a full-scale service on a festive occasion. Both are bright, major-key settings, apt for voices in the *pergola* and the *pulpitum* where so many of the so-called "double-choir" works were given.[15] Several of these *cori spezzati* psalms were obscured in the score arrangement published in 1940, but they have been revised for the 1999 edition.

The smaller-scale psalms sung in the Doge's private chapel required only a group of soloists and organ. This is also true of the hymns, the second *Magnificat* and the three settings of *Salve Regina,* which can best be performed by soloists.

---

14. Cited by Paolo Fabbri, *Inediti Monteverdiani.*

15. Although David Bryant's path-breaking study of the true nature and effect of divided choirs ends before the Monteverdian period, its investigation of the earlier years is unrivalled. See "The 'Cori Spezzati' of St Mark's: Myth and Reality," in *Early Music History* 1 (1981): 165–86.

In a niche of its own stands the formidable eight-part *Magnificat,* surely one of the composer's great masterpieces. Like the *Credo* it is defective, but not so much as to prevent the reconstruction of two missing voice parts. It is almost certainly a late work, produced under stress, since the orchestral contribution was obviously added by an incompetent assistant. Some far from acceptable sections in the violin parts call for drastic revision. The melodic link between the end of an antiphon for Christmas Vespers (*Hodie Christus natus est*), Epiphany (*Tribus miraculis*), Ascension (*O Rex gloriae*), or Purification (*Senex puerum portabat*) and the opening four-note motive of the actual canticle probably show that the work was associated with those feasts, all of them important in the liturgical calendar. Monteverdi must have used this setting on many occasions. The explanation of the error-filled violin parts is that the wrong set was sent to Magni for setting up and printing.

The psalm *Memento Domine David* can be linked to a feast whose celebration connects with one of the composer's assignments outside S. Marco. It is part of the liturgy for St. John Baptist. We should praise those who kept diaries, for on June 24, 1620, a diary-keeping diplomat from the Low Countries, visiting Venice with a group of friends, heard that Monteverdi himself would be directing music at a church then known as S. Giovanni del Rialto—or S. Giovanni Nuovo, because it had been carefully restored some hundred years previously after a disastrous fire. It was actually dedicated not to St. John the Baptist, but to S. Giovanni Elemosinario (the Almsgiver).

The diplomat Constantijn Huyghens misheard the name as "Saint Jean et Lucie," an excusable phonetic rendering of "Elemosinario." The feast being celebrated was not that of the Almsgiver but of the prophet. Huyghens wrote in his diary:

> On June 24, the Feast of St. John Baptist, I was taken to the church of [S. Giovanni Elemosinario] where I heard the most excellent music that I think I shall ever hear in my life. The renowned Claudio Monteverdi, who composed it, supervised, and conducted it on this occasion, had an accompaniment of four theorboes, two cornetti, two bassoons, two violins, a bass viol of enormous size, organs and other instruments, all of which were managed and played superbly well, with ten or twelve voices in addition. I was quite beside myself with delight.[16]

---

16. Huygens, 128–29.

A passage from *Dixit Dominus* in the 1999 edition and in the 1940 edition

The psalms proper for this feast were *Dixit, Confitebor, Beatus vir, Laudate pueri,* and *Memento Domine David,* the last-mentioned being included in only one of Monteverdi's publications—the *Selva.* For the same feast and perhaps for the same occasion, he wrote a motet for St. John Baptist, *Fuge anima mea,* published in 1620.

When the long line of liturgical compositions comes to an end, there remains but one work, the contrafactum of his *Lament of Arianna.* By far his most famous song, it had even been published without the composer's name, and would eventually reappear as part of a revived production of the opera in 1639, just at the crucial moment when the *Selva* was going to press. Should he close the harmonious tribute to Eleonora with a deferential "moral bow" to her and to the Virgin Mary? The question had come to mind again when he wrote to Giovanni Battista Doni on October 22, 1633:

> when I was about to compose the "Lament of Arianna," finding no book that could show me the natural way of imitation, not even one that would explain how I ought to have been an imitator, I found (let me tell you) what hard work I had to do in order to achieve the little I did do in the way of imitation, and I therefore hope it is not going to be displeasing.[17]

In any event, he asked an ecclesiastical colleague to write a *Pianto della Madonna* in Latin prose, making it fit the music. Although it hardly ranks as one of his most inspired works, it may stand as a finale reflecting duty and honor in equal proportions.

> . . . but let it come out as it will: in the end I shall be happier to be moderately praised in the new style, than greatly praised in the ordinary; and for this further presumption I ask fresh pardon.[18]

THE LITURGICAL YEAR IN VENICE

For the last thirty years of his life, Monteverdi was in Venice, and of those years he spent many preparing for the publication of his *Selva.* While there was much in the city to encourage him—the ceaseless counterpoint of musical life, with its services in churches,

17. Letter no. 124, 22 October 1633.
18. Ibid.

monasteries and *scuole,* not to mention the throbbing presses of
Vincenti and Magni—certain drawbacks stimulated the victim-
complex which had already established itself as a guiding element
in his nature. After living in the city for nearly three years, he told
Ferdinando Gonzaga of his fears and qualms:

> The very great need in which I find myself, Most Serene Lord, having
> necessarily to provide my poor house with bread, wine, and many other
> things; and being impoverished mainly by having to educate my sons
> (born and bred over in Mantua) for whom, on account of the dangerous
> liberty here in Venice, I have been bound to maintain a tutor.[19]

So despite a general improvement in his lifestyle, a number of day-
to-day problems remained.

He was spurred on as much by the constant procession of festivals within S. Marco (or connected with it by ancient and external
links) as by the golden opportunities to compose and conduct music
for the *scuole* and city churches that numbered 120 or more. Sansovino, who counted the organs, said there were 144, a number that
is nearly confirmed by the English visitor Thomas Coryate, who
guessed 143. Over and beyond the festivals, the *andate,* and the occasional or ceremonial event, there is no doubt that music—which
usually included the *maestro di capella*—played an important part
in celebrations for a new procurator, *primicerius,* patriarch or doge.

Those who believe that funerals involved a minimal musical contribution should glance at an account of the funeral of Cosimo II
Grand Duke of Tuscany, which took place at SS. Giovanni e Paolo
on May 25, 1621. Published in Venice by Ciotti, Giulio Strozzi's
text mentions many lengthy works, some of them composed by
Monteverdi. Their composition and rehearsal must have cost him
many days of work and worry.

When two of Cosimo's sons attended a banquet given for them
at the Arsenale in 1628 by the Doge Giovanni Cornaro, all five of
them were celebrated in five sonnets by the faithful Giulio Strozzi
and set to music by Monteverdi, who doubtless availed himself of
a five-part musical texture. Although the music of *I cinque fratelli*
is lost, the poet's amusing verses remain.[20]

---

19. Letter no. 18, 27 July 1616.
20. Venezia: Deuchino, 1628. I am grateful to my daughter Daphne Stevens
Pascucci for transcribing this poem in Florence.

> To impoverish Lake Garda of famous fish,
> to clear the sea around us of unique shells
> and from that sea, where day doth gain its life,
> to carry off the golden gifts of Bacchus,
>
> Thou hast done well, O Adria. Wherefore thou art prized
> for achieving it in a great banquet;
> but enjoying this in thy liquid realm
> does not appeal to outstanding royalty.
>
> The gentle desire which leads them
> to search for countries so varied, and so many,
> has Discipline and Honesty as Leader.
>
> On thy temperate and holy customs,
> and on the ancient valor which shines again in thee,
> two eager wanderers feed their eyes.

The final line is then repeated to form the opening of the second sonnet—a formula to which, in a more general sense, Monteverdi became accustomed in his Venetian involvements; for as soon as one project ended, another began. Whether he ever found time for a holiday on the Lido is anybody's guess, yet he certainly had friends there, for Abbot Angelo Grillo stayed for some years at S. Nicolo, one of the "due castelli" (the other being S. Andrea) that framed the annual Feast of the Ascension.

Whether he thought deeply about musical theory is also debatable. His two letters to G. B. Doni in 1633–34 and slightly later the Preface to *Madrigali guerrieri et amorosi* indicate that he devoted leisure to it in his more mature years. But he was first and foremost a practical musician and only incidentally a writer about the theory and aesthetics of his art.

Marco Boschini, who contributed so much towards the appreciation of art in Venice, commented in his *Carta del Navegar Pitoresco* with remarkable sensitivity on Bernardo Strozzi's portrait of Monteverdi. He was lavish too in his praise of Venice and its painterly properties:

> Truly this island is a jewel,
> set in the crystal sea that surrounds it;
> where the wave beats flux and reflux,
> doesn't it seem as if it's done with a brush?[21]

---

21. *La Carta del Navegar Pitoresco* (Venezia: Baba, 1660).

For a man recently arrived from the landlocked marshlands of Mantua, Venice was more than a jewel set in a crystal sea: it was a new musical planet steeped in an old tradition reaching back to composers such as Antonio Romano, Christoforo de Monte, or Johannes Ciconia, who sang the praises of successive doges from the dawn of the fifteenth century. It had moreover opened wide its treasury to supply Monteverdi not only with a salary that would finally do him justice, but with a generous provision for a glorious musical establishment:

> this Most Serene Republic has never before given to any of my predecessors—whether it were Adriano or Cipriano or Zarlino, or anyone else—but 200 ducats in salary, whereas to me they give 400; a favor that ought not to be so lightly set aside by me without some consideration, since (Most Illustrious Lord) this Most Serene Signory does not make an innovation without very careful thought, wherefore (I repeat) this particular favor ought to command my utmost respect.[22]

In Mantua the pressure of duties in 1607 and 1608 had nearly destroyed him, whereas in Venice

> the duties are very light, since the whole choir is liable to discipline except the Director of Music—in fact, it is in his hands, having a singer censured or excused and giving leave or not; and if he does not go into chapel, nobody says anything. Moreover his allowance is assured until his death: neither the death of a procurator nor that of a doge interferes with it, and by always serving faithfully and with reverence he has greater expectations, not the opposite; and as regards his salary money, if he does not go at the appointed time to pick it up, it is brought round to his house.[23]

If this were the fundamental gift of a grateful city to a hard-working composer, he could look forward to even further sources of income:

> Then there is the occasional, which consists of whatever extra I can easily earn outside S. Marco of about 200 ducats a year (invited as I am again and again by the wardens of the guilds), because whoever can engage the director to look after their music—not to mention the payment of 30 ducats, and even 40, and up to 50 for two vespers and a

---

22. Letter no. 49, 13 March 1620.
23. Ibid.

Mass—does not fail to take him on, and they also thank him afterwards with well-chosen words.[24]

Seven years later Monteverdi offered a further and similar comparison to the same recipient—Alessandro Striggio—and, even though this correspondence would be cut short by the count's death in 1631, whoever reads between the lines will realize that both held firm beliefs and principles, notwithstanding almost thirty years of friendship and many opportunities to collaborate. After a plea for a canonry from Cremona, the composer turned again to Venice and the security of his employment:

> I am certainly not rich, but neither am I poor; moreover I lead a life with a certain security of income until my death, and furthermore I am always absolutely sure of always having it on the appointed pay-days, which come every two months without fail. Indeed, if it is the least bit late, they send it to my house. Then as regards chapel I do as I wish, since there is the sub-director, called Assistant Director of Music, and there is no obligation to teach. Also, the city is most beautiful, and if I want to put myself to minimal trouble, I come up with a further 200 good ducats. Such is my condition.[25]

He appreciated his surroundings and loved his work. Even if something went wrong in his life, sixty-six golden ducats would be his every two months. Undoubtedly he worked harder than usual for major feasts, but since there is no trace of at least two dozen Christmas Masses, they could be lost or on the other hand they might (like *La finta pazza Licori*) never have been written. Outside commissions impinged on his work for S. Marco, but he usually gave first place to his official duties, even if it meant that outsiders had to wait:

> This delay on my part came about because of the hard work that had to be done on the Mass for Christmas Eve, for what with composing it and copying it out, I had to give up the entire month of December, almost without a break.[26]

The doge's first *andata* after Christmas took place on the Vigil of the Purification. On the eve of February 2nd he went to visit the

24. Ibid.
25. Letter no. 106, 10 September 1627.
26. Letter no. 20, 29 December 1616.

church of Santa Maria Formosa to honor the promise made to the guild of *Casselleri* (makers of marriage-coffers) who in the mid-tenth century had rescued a group of Venetian girls—on the way to get married—from a shipful of marauding Dalmatian sailors. When the doge and procession arrived at the church, a solemn Mass was sung. Although there is no mention of polyphony in Monteverdi's day, it would be surprising if there were none. On the day of the feast, the musicians were at their appointed places in S. Marco:

> and when the procession has reached the choir, the ordinary benediction of candles is made by the celebrant of the principal Mass, who is always a canon of the church.[27]

A few weeks later the feast of the Annunciation (March 25) called for a sung Mass and Compline. In the case of the *andata* to S. Giorgio Maggiore, the liturgy became slightly more complex, since the body of St. Stephen had been removed there in the twelfth century. This meant that the doge and signoria had to cross and recross the lagoon for Vespers and Mass:

> then they left, and went in the doge's boats to S. Giorgio to hear Mass, which was said by the abbot there and sung by the musicians of S. Marco.[28]

The greatest and most colorful of the springtime *andate,* that of S. Marco, took place on April 25, beginning on the previous evening when Vespers were sung:

> Its festival was then celebrated with the greatest solemnity: inasmuch as the extent of the great choir being made ready by the Signoria at First Vespers of the Vigil and the Republic's treasure of jewels placed on the main altar by the procurator who was Treasurer of the church in that year, the great chapter of canons of S. Marco with a smaller group of minor canons and other priests serving the church went forward with the cross before them, all clad in copes and with silver candlesticks, meeting at the foot of the Scala dei Giganti, the Doge and Signoria, who descended with all the triumphs; and the canons went before, coming out of the principal door of the palace towards the entrance of the church; and on reaching the high altar the vicar of the canons, wearing a precious crimson satin cope with golden embroidery and pearls,

---

27. Sansovino, *Venetia città nobilissima* (Venezia: 1663), 493.
28. Sansovino, 504.

stopped with two canons on each side, and when the Doge had reached
his throne and all the Signoria their places he intoned Vespers which
was sung by the musicians with all possible solemnity; and the ritual
being ended the Doge lit a candle in a silver candlestick held in his hand
while the Magnificat was sung, a gift and privilege granted him by Pope
Alexander III.[29]

Monteverdi makes an early reference to the Easter ceremonies in a
letter to Striggio, stressing the fact that the responsibility is by no
means a light one:

> Since Your Lordship grants me the boon of a little time to write the
> music for Your Lordship's most beautiful words, I shall accept the favor,
> because of the many duties I shall have at S. Marco during the Holy
> Week, and also because of the feast-days, which for the Director of
> Music are by no means few in times like this.[30]

The extent of the choir's involvement as described in accounts of
the ceremonies also reveals the onerous tasks of the director of
music. Palm Sunday, which called for the accustomed processions
and motets, also demanded a certain agility on the part of singers
ascending *in eminentiori loco:*

> the procession having arrived before the great door of the church, the
> crucifer halts at the little steps of the first door. The priests do the same,
> and before the door they form a choir, the Doge and Signoria also stop-
> ping there. This done, the singers who have already climbed through the
> corridors of the church up to the four golden horses, begin at once to
> sing those beautiful verses by Bishop Theodulph of Orleans, "Gloria,
> laus, et honor" and those which follow, as approved by holy church.
> Meanwhile when this is ended, the chorus of priests in the piazza repeat
> the same. Many young children who are used to the trick are on top of
> the church roof, and throw down various kinds of live birds, large and
> small, some of them with mitres of painted paper attached to their feet
> to prevent them from flying too far, and these come down into the pi-
> azza, and those who catch them can keep them and eat them for Easter.[31]

As Holy Week unfolded its crescendo of sorrows in daily offices
shorn of instrumental participation, the choir and its director were

---

29. Ibid., 507.
30. Letter no. 32, 7 March 1619.
31. Sansovino, 518.

in constant service. On Wednesday a procession in barges ended near S. Giovanni Elemosinario (S. Giovanni di Rialto) where the people received indulgences,

and then coming into S. Marco, the Doge hears the divine offices, the three lessons of the first nocturn being sung with a sad chant by the musicians of the church, the three others of the second nocturn by three minor canons, and those of the third by three canons, deputed to do this by the director of music.[32]

On Holy Thursday Mass was sung by the choir, but Vespers was said. Good Friday witnessed the distribution of sixty candles of purest wax to the six great *scuole,* and the formation of a procession bearing the Sacrament to the Sepulchre;

Then follow the clergy of the church, after whom came the singers divided into two choirs; then four men who carry four lighted candles . . . and the Most Holy Body of Christ having reached the door of the sacristy, a chorus of singers all kneeling down sing *Venite adoremus,* and all that follows; and the other choir replies *Popule meus, quid feci tibi?* with the other verses.[33]

The choir sang, as the service progressed, *Cum autem pervenisset ad locum,* and *Sepulto Domino.* A solemn *Te Deum* and Mass followed on Holy Saturday, when there was a pause during which everyone prepared for Easter Day. On this great feast the entire musical establishment was bound to take part. Since the *Pala d'Oro* was opened, the liturgy was sung with double choir, which normally involved the use of many areas in the basilica, especially the galleries, since the vast congregation took up all the floor space:

On this day the choir and the Doge's throne are prepared, and the golden altar frontal being opened, the procurator of the church who is the Treasurer in that year places the treasure on the altar.[34]

The morning continued with a solemn Mass, followed by the *andata* to San Zaccaria for Vespers.

---

32. Ibid., 519.
33. Ibid., 520.
34. Ibid., 521.

Having heard the sermon in S. Marco, the Doge leaves in triumph and is led with the Signoria to the aforementioned church. He is received there with ceremony by the nuns and Abbess, and a most solemn Vespers is sung.[35]

It was not only to Striggio that Monteverdi made Easter excuses. He mentioned them in a letter to Prince Vincenzo Gonzaga:

But let Your Lordship take note: throughout Holy Week I am at S. Marco, and the three feast-days likewise. As soon as they are over, you will not see the following Saturday without my sending satisfaction.[36]

Two feasts in May could have been influenced by Easter from year to year: the Finding of the Holy Cross (May 3), and the Ascension, forty days after Easter. Again to Prince Vincenzo, Monteverdi writes of the arrangements in S. Marco for the Holy Cross ceremonies and pleads for more time in which to complete *Andromeda*:

on Thursday week, which is Holy Cross Day, the Most Holy Blood will be displayed, and I shall have to be ready with a concerted Mass, and motets for the entire day, inasmuch as it will also be displayed throughout the day on an altar in the middle of S. Marco, set up high especially.[37]

The close succession of liturgical feasts in 1618 gave the composer an advantage which he unhesitatingly pressed home, for no sooner was Holy Cross day over than plans had to be made for Ascension. On this day, all Venice took to the lagoon in a vast fleet of colorful vessels of every size and variety, the doge and signoria in the majestic Bucintoro and the populace in the most suitable boats they could find. The naval battle in 1177 when Pietro Ziani, son of the doge, overcame Frederic Barbarossa's fleet and forced the emperor to do homage to Pope Alexander III, had been a crucial episode in Venetian history.

On Ascension Day every year the *andata* reached the far-off part of the lagoon near the "due castelli," S. Andrea and S. Nicolò, where the seal-entry to the city provided an appropriate background for the ceremony, part religious and part historical. Although the

---

35. Ibid., 495.
36. Letter no. 33, 22 March 1619.
37. Letter no. 29, 21 April 1618.

throwing of a golden ring into the water symbolized the wedding of city and sea from ancient times, it is from later accounts that we learn the role played by music:

> On this *andata,* and on the return, the musicians of S. Marco sing in the middle of the journey some beautiful motet.[38]

Monteverdi stresses the importance of the feast and its demands on him and the musicians in his charge:

> I shall have to rehearse a certain cantata in praise of His Serenity, which is designed to be sung every year in the Bucintoro [the doge's ceremonial boat] when, with all the Signoria, he attends the wedding of the sea on Ascension Day, and I must also rehearse a Mass and solemn Vespers, which is sung in S. Marco on such an occasion, and so—My Most illustrious Lord—I am afraid I cannot do what I would like.[39]

The cantata was clearly a secular piece in the style of *Quattro Dee che'l mondo onora,* by his predecessor Baldassare Donato, while the sung Mass at S. Nicolò del Lido and the solemn vespers in S. Marco would make use of a large ensemble of singers and players.

Had an enemy wished to humiliate Monteverdi in the worst possible way, he would have chosen an occasion such as the *Sensa,* and this in fact was the course followed in June 1623 when an anonymous evildoer dropped a letter into the *bocca del leone* near the Doge's palace. Directed to the State Inquisitor, this document could have sent the composer into prison or exile. Since five-sixths of the administration had to find the accusation well-founded but nothing happened, it is clear that the plot failed. The denunciation mentioned disloyalty to the Republic, supporting the Habsburgs, using profane language and making a mistake while directing the music for Vespers of the Ascension.

> Item: at the time of the indulgences at Ascensiontide, he made a most notable error in chapel, in the *pergola* at Vespers; and afterwards when admonished for the error he said: "I shit on the clergy and I don't care how many priests are here. To hell with them—I am Claudio."[40]

---

38. Sansovino, 501.
39. Letter no. 29, 21 April 1618.
40. Venezia, Archivio de Stato, Inquisitori di Stato, Busta 643, Riferti dei Confidenti, senza data (cited in Glixon, *Traitor*).

The language is suspiciously like Domenico Aldegati's, as quoted in Monteverdi's only letter from 1637:

> and I shit on him and whoever protects him, and so that everyone can understand me, I say that Claudio Monteverdi is a thieving fucking he-goat.[41]

Aldegati had been a tiresome trouble-maker since 1614–15, when he was responsible for unrest among the basilica singers. Enemies of this kind had bothered Monteverdi since his boyhood, for his earliest publication mentions envious detractors in its preface:

> You therefore will be the one to protect me from the evil tongues of detractors and envious men, who are accustomed to work against those who aspire by ceaseless work and study to earn immortality through their own virtue and so acquire a treasure more precious than anything.[42]

As in Cremona, so in Mantua and Venice. Leaving the city of the Gonzaga after years of service from which he earned only a few scudi, he was robbed even of that by blackguards almost certainly hired by the treasury staff of whom he so often complained. Even today one drives through Sanguinetto half-expecting that some mishap might occur. In his youth he faced jealousy, in middle age attacks by ruffians, and in what should have been his serene years the shrill screams of enmity echoed around the basilica he served so faithfully.

Despite the inconvenience of summer heat and insects (of which Dr. Burney complained in 1770), musical life in July continued at an often feverish pace. On July 17 there would be Vespers for the Carmelites in their fourteenth-century church near the Calle Lunga S. Barnaba:

> I then had to go—pressed by the entreaties of many friends—to the Carmelite Church, as it was the day of First Vespers of the Most Holy Madonna of that Order, and stay there fully occupied until almost 7 P.M.[43]

On the third Sunday in July an *andata* to the Chiesa del Redentore on the Giudecca took place. This festival, instituted by Doge

---

41. Letter no. 126, 9 June 1637.
42. Preface to *Sacrae Cantiunculae* (Venezia: Angelo Gardano, 1582).
43. Letter no. 101, 24 July 1627.

Luigi Mocenigo in 1577, took the form of a thanksgiving after the plague. It is one of the very few to survive today from the time of the Republic. The Redentore was in the hands of Capuchin friars:

> after hearing Low Mass said by the prior of those fathers, and motets sung by the musicians of S. Marco at the Offertory and the Elevation, he returned to S. Marco for High Mass.[44]

Still not over-anxious to travel to Mantua, the composer reinforced his reluctance by referring to the *andata* in a letter to Striggio:

> I shall be staying here not so much because the occasion (as indeed you hint) is not now so urgent, but because the task has been given me of serving this Most Serene Republic tomorrow, which will be the 20th of this month, at the Church of Our Redeemer, a day celebrated by this Most Serene Republic in memory of a favor received from the hand of God, which was the liberation of the city from a terrible plague.[45]

Two notable and neighboring feasts were the Assumption of the Virgin on August 15 and S. Rocco (supposed to provide protection against the plague) on August 16, when the Scuola di San Rocco added its own musical contribution to the main event. This included a procession to the church where the saint was buried, just between the Frari and what is now the Archivio di Stato. Outstanding concerts were well established there long before Monteverdi's arrival, as may be seen from the description in Thomas Coryate's *Crudities,* which tells of the festivities of 1608. Two decades later, Monteverdi was in charge.

On September 8 the *andata* in honor of the Nativity of the Virgin took place, but its splendor was far surpassed by the procession to the nunnery of S. Giustina near the Fondamenta Nuove on October 7. The doge and his immense retinue left the Molo and proceeded to the Rio S. Lorenzo, turning across the island to the Rio S. Giustina. On this day not only were the liturgical feasts of S. Giustina and the Madonna del Rosario celebrated, but the anniversary of the Battle of Lepanto in 1571, when powerful Venetian galleys defeated the Turks.

> The Doge and the Signoria travel in flat-bottomed boats, and after hearing Mass sung by one of his canons with great solemnity of vocal and

---

44. Sansovino, 513.
45. Letter no. 58, 19 July 1620.

instrumental music provided by the musicians of S. Marco before an astonishing number of people, he goes back to S. Marco where the great confraternities pass by; and the monks and nuns, and the assemblies of priests, having passed through the Choir on the way to S. Giustina, the Doge goes back to his palace.[46]

A reminder of this festivity emerges from Monteverdi's letter to the Marchese Enzo Bentivoglio in Ferrara, who had sent an intermezzo to be set to music for future celebrations in Parma. The composer returned from Chioggia later than expected and begged for extra time.

. . . this brief lapse of time occurring against my will, I wanted to ask Your Excellency to be so kind as to give me leave to remain in Venice until the 7th of next month, for on that day the Most Serene Doge goes in procession to S. Giustina to thank God our Saviour for the joyous naval victory. He is accompanied by the entire Senate, and solemn music is sung.[47]

Certain processions and ceremonies of a temporary nature were not repeated from year to year. So many of the inhabitants of the city had died in the first four months of the plague that the doge promulgated a vow to the Virgin: a new church was to be built and dedicated to her as Santa Maria della Salute. The cornerstone would be laid at a site near the Dogana on October 26, 1630. Monteverdi and the choir of S. Marco were certainly present at the ceremony, which is fully described in official documents.

His Serenity with the Signoria and all the Senate went into S. Marco, and when everyone was at his place there began the Litany of the B. V. M. for two choirs, and the procession passed through the door which goes under the portico of the palace, bearing the image of the Virgin painted by S. Luca.[48]

Inspired by the same awesome topic, the next *andata* on November 21 combined the office for the Presentation of the Virgin in the Temple with general rejoicing at the end of the plague. Until this moment the feast had been classed as a Duplex; but the additional

46. Sansovino, 514.

47. Letter no. 111, 23 Sept 1627, to Enzo Bentivoglio.

48. Venezia, Archivio di Stato, Collegio, Ceremoniali III, f. 71v, cited by James Moore: *Venezia favorita da Maria* . . . , 319.

weight of this new ceremony brought with it a great change: Doge Nicolò Contarini ordered the opening of the *Pala d'Oro* and performance of the liturgy by double choir. After Contarini's death his successor Francesco Erizzo confirmed the order in 1631, which was duly noted by the master of ceremonies:

> Doge Francesco Erizzo ordered me to open the altar frontal on the Feast of the Presentation, which is sung by two choirs.[49]

The section given up to Christmas in S. Marco is the only one to mention composers by name: Croce, Gabrieli, and Bassano. Giovanni Croce became director of music at the basilica in 1603 and died in 1609; Giovanni Gabrieli was appointed to the second organ in 1584, dying in 1612, and Giovanni Bassano served as director of concerts with the organ from 1601 until 1617. They coincided as a team only from 1601 until 1609, a period of eight years when Stringa made his revision of Sansovino in 1604. He refers to the three as "directors and leaders," and in fact Bassano's title was "capo dei concerti dell'organo." The chapter heading *Andate diverse in certi giorni dell'anno* provides information derived from Sansovino, Stringa and Martinioni, and the description begins with a lavish account of the music at Christmas Vespers:

> at nearly 4 o'clock in the afternoon the Doge came down into the church where he was joined by the Vicar, accompanied by four minor canons, and began Vespers which with choral music and the sweetest sounds was sung by the regular musicians of S. Marco and by others hired especially to make up a larger number, because on that evening they sang in eight, ten, twelve and sixteen choirs to the astonishment and amazement of all, and above all of the foreigners who admitted that they had never heard music more rare and more singular in any part of the world; and they speak the truth, for the musicians, vocal as well as instrumental, are most excellent, having notably for their directors and leaders those three famous young men, Croce (called Il Chiozotto), Gabrieli and Bassano.[50]

Monteverdi's first mention of Christmas music is found at the beginning of a letter dated 1619 to Striggio:

---

49. Venezia, Biblioteca Nazionale Marciana, Cod. lat. III 172 f.51.
50. Sansovino, 516.

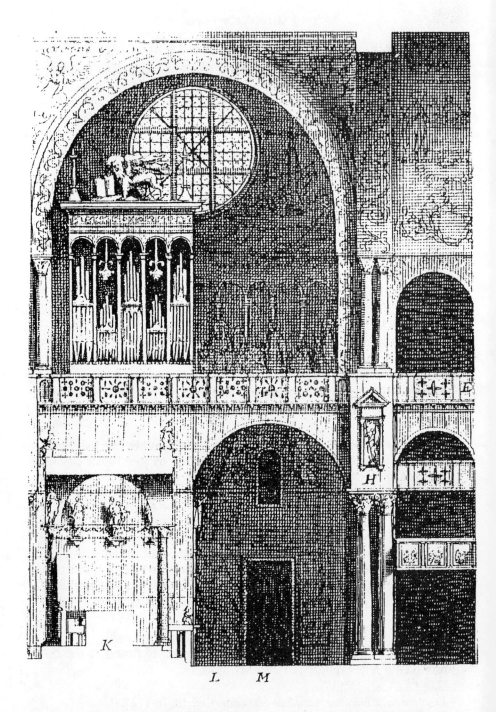

Engraving from Antonio Zatta, *Ducale Basilica de S. Marco,* **showing organ and** *pergola*

L

Without fail, once the feast of Christmas is over, I shall devote all the time ahead of me to Your Lordship's service.[51]

It is mentioned again in 1627 in a letter from Parma to Enzo Bentivoglio:

Nor have I so far neglected to do some work on the tourney, and since at any rate the greater part—if not all of it—is planned, I would like to have leave to be able to go to Venice to attend to my duties on Christmas Eve at S. Marco, since this solemn feast is the greatest that the Director of Music has in the entire year.[52]

Monteverdi's career was inextricably tied to the liturgical year at San Marco and to the ceaseless round of extracurricular duties in Venice, Mantua, Parma, Bologna or wherever his widespread fame beckoned. A vicemaestro was of course always present to assist him, and for the first six years he enjoyed the help of Marc'Antonio Negri (a pioneer in the composition of trio sonatas), who published an impressive set of psalms in the very year of the maestro's arrival. From 1620 until 1626 Alessandro Grandi served as Monteverdi's aide—a gifted composer subsequently invited to S. Maria Maggiore in Bergamo as director of music. Grandi's successor, Giovanni Rovetta, a virtuoso player of wind and stringed instruments as well as a prolific composer and a priest, ranked as one of Monteverdi's most successful pupils.

Nevertheless he stood as his own man, accepting occasional help but discouraging frequent interference. Although many composers of the stature of Negri, Grandi and Rovetta could be found, there was only one Monteverdi.

PERFORMANCE PRACTICE

The passing-bell of the sixteenth century paradoxically rang in the birth of the *basso continuo*. Madrigals for voices and harpsichord by Luzzasco Luzzaschi appear in 1601 and a sacred collection for voices and organ by Ludovico Viadana sounded forth in 1602. But if Luzzaschi's elegant volume of virtuoso masterpieces was never reprinted, Viadana's varied collection of motets proved

---

51. Letter no. 35, 13 December 1619.
52. Letter no. 113, 30 October 1627.

to be a financial boon for its publisher Vincenti, who issued several reprints in its first ten years.

This vital new musical principle brilliantly exploited in two different fields came to exert a profound effect on Monteverdi, who had known Viadana at the cathedral in Mantua and was certainly acquainted with Luzzaschi, whose name he mentioned in a letter to Annibale Chieppio.[53]

The fifteen years of Viadana's residence in Mantua coincided with and somewhat overlapped Monteverdi's time there. By 1596 Viadana had become a Franciscan friar, his interest in courtly music almost exhausted, but in church music of all kinds he remained industrious and prolific. Traveling widely, he published and conducted his own compositions, living as inexpensively as a friar might while at the same time keeping constantly busy with his pen. After spending only six months at the seaside town of Concordia (the old Roman encampment of Concordia Juliana just south of Portogruaro), he moved down the eastern coast to the city of Fano, its twelfth-century cathedral providing an ample setting for his new wave of music for many choirs. This he quickly perfected after 1609, publishing it as his *Salmi a Quattro Chori con Organo* in 1612, exactly one year before Monteverdi arrived in Venice.

Shaken to the core by his experiences on the road from Mantua, Monteverdi reached S. Marco only to find a vastly complex liturgy and the occasional need to compose music for four choirs. His great publication of 1610 had proved him capable of working fluently in a double-choir format, yet the basilica required music on an even grander scale. Nevertheless here at one of his own publishing houses he found a set of polychoral psalms by an old acquaintance from Mantua, and the preface could not have been written more clearly:

> The first chorus, for five voices, will be placed with the main organ and will be the favored one. It will be sung and musically declaimed by five good singers who must be reliable, clear, and capable of singing in the modern style.
>
> In this choir there will be no instrument other than the organ, and an archlute if you want it. The organist will be careful to see to the registration at the right place, and in time, and when he sees the words "empty" and "full" he must register empty [bass only] or full.

---

53. Letter no. 6, 2 December 1608.

When one two, three, four or five voices sing in this choir, the organist will always play simply and reliably, neither adding ornaments nor
making passage-work of any kind. But in ripieno passages he will play
as he wishes because then it is his turn.

The second chorus, for four voices, will be the main body, where one
finds all the muscle and foundation of good music. In this choir there
should be no less than sixteen singers, for with less than that number
the tutti will always sound feeble; but when there are twenty or thirty
both of voices and instruments, it will be a good musical ensemble and
will succeed best of all.

The third choir, in four parts, will be high: the top line, being the
highest, will be played by the cornetto or violin. The second will be
sung by a better soprano, or by two or three. The alto is a mezzo-soprano, and will be sung by several voices and violins and curved cornetti. The tenor will also be sung by several voices, with trombones and
double basses, or organ at the higher octave.

The fourth choir, for four voices, will be low; that is to say for equal
voices. The top line, which is a very low alto, will be sung by several
voices, with violins at the octave and curved cornetti. The alto is a very
comfortable tenor, and will be sung by several voices with trombones.
The tenor, or baritone (that is, half-bass) must also be accompanied by
good voices, or by trombone and double basses. The bass is always
deep, and must be sung by low basses with double trombones and
basses and bassoons, the organ being at the octave below.[54]

The second part offers suggestions for polychoral settings ranging
from two to eight choirs, the term "choir" in this context referring
also to small groups of perhaps four performers, to be accommo-
dated in some prestigious niche and serving mainly to increase the
scale of wonderment. In the city of Monteverdi's birth there would
be motets for six choirs in 1616 by Rodiano Barera and Tarquinio
Merula,[55] while Martinioni, as we have seen, could envisage even
sixteen choirs at S. Marco.

The task of the maestro di capella is to keep an eye on the basso
continuo part, set the tempo, and cue the solo voices and ensembles,
looking straight at the choirs and raising both hands as the signal

54. Viadana, Preface to *Salmi a Quattro Chori* (Venezia: Vincenti, 1612). Certain minor composers (Fergusio, *Motetti e Dialoghi,* 1612; Donati, *Sacri con-
centus,* 1612) also entertained comparable and contemporaneous ideas on
polychoral practice. See Denis Arnold, "Monteverdi's Church Music: Some Venetian Traits," *Monthly Musical Record* 83 (1958): 83–91.

55. Giuseppe Pontiroli, "Notizie di musicisti cremonesi dei secoli XVI e
XVII," *Bollettino Storico Cremonese* 22 (1961–64): 169, 175.

for a tutti. The warning to avoid excessive rests and contrapuntal complications recalls Monteverdi's strictures on the tiresome texture of Galeazzo Sirena's motets as described in a letter of 1609.[56] The mention of consecutive octaves in a sixteen-voice work by Pallavicino ought not to surprise us.

> These psalms can also be sung by two choirs only: that is, first and second choirs. Whoever wants to give us a fine example, as pleases the world today, in 4, 5, 6, 7 and 8 choirs, let him double the second, third and fourth choir as he wishes, without any fear of going wrong. The entire operation depends on the said first choir, for five voices, singing well.
>
> The director of music will be in that same choir of five voices, always watching the organist's Basso Continuo so as to guide the progress of the music, and signifying where a solo voice has to sing, or two or three or four or five. And when the Ripieno sections occur he will turn his face to all the choirs, raising both his hands, to indicate that all sing together.
>
> All the choirs on their own account sing according to what is correct, and all have their harmonies, and separated one from the other cannot tell whether they are singing at the octave or in unison. This is the way I have been pleased to do it since the music succeeds somewhat better, for whoever wants to arrange it traditionally has to make use of pauses, half-pauses, crotchet rests, points and syncopations. This makes the music distorted, rustic and pig-headed, rushing along at breakneck speed and with little grace.
>
> Nevertheless I know that you will find some wit and, professing a delicate and refined ear, will take some care about this novelty; although others have done the same before me, as indeed you can see in the printed *Jubilate* and *Laudate* for sixteen voices by Pallavicino, where the sopranos and tenors sing for 25 or 30 bars in octaves by conjunct motion. But, to finish, I have done this in my own way and others can do likewise, since we are now at a juncture where whoever does worse appears to do better. And God be with you![57]

Fra Ludovico has already recommended that the maestro keep his eyes on the figured bass part, and although this was often printed it should be borne in mind that manuscript parts were by no means unknown. Several references to these occur in seventeenth-century documents at Cremona specifically mentioning Monteverdi:

56. Letter no. 8, 10 September 1609.
57. Viadana, *Salmi* (1612).

His printed and manuscript works circulated among musicians allow them to see what may be best and most rare in that art.[58]

There was also a pre-manuscript stage of writing which is too little understood to be passed over, for Monteverdi undoubtedly made use of it in his younger days. This required the composer to set down his musical ideas on a slate or paper, instantly erasable, from which copies in ink could subsequently be made. Cipriano de Rore's cartella brought forth this affirmation by Luzzaschi:

> I, Luzzasco Luzzaschi, citizen of Ferrara, bear witness that this folio belonged to the very famous and most excellent Cipriano Rore, Flemish musician and Director of Music of the late Most Excellent Lord Duke Ercole d'Este of Ferrara. On this folio he wrote the compositions first thought out in his mind, as was his custom. I being his pupil at that time saw him writing on the said folio the Gloria of a Mass which he wrote in Ferrara and other compositions of his written at various times. And he gave this folio to me when he left here in 1557, together with the attached Miserere which he wrote in Flanders when he was a young man; and now I present it to the Most Illustrious and Most Reverend Lord Cardinal Borromeo my most esteemed lord and master, affirming what I have said on being the truth. I Luzzasco Luzzaschi have written this present testimony with my own hand, in Ferrara on September 29, 1606.[59]

The use of both a *cartella* and a manuscript copy shows us that if much music of the past has been lost, there are rational ways of explaining it. But once the basso continuo had been copied from the *cartella,* or printed as one of a set of parts, the director could use it as a guide or *aide-mémoire* to the music. No score was necessary, since he knew the entries by heart.

In fact the entire art of direction, although buried in the memory, could be resurrected immediately by the act of rehearsal. Walter Porter, who studied with Monteverdi in 1616 or thereabouts, wrote the book *Mottets of Two Voyces,* which was published in 1659. The address "to all Lovers of Musick" in the copy at Christ Church Library, Oxford, has a few words added by hand to the printed page, very probably by Porter or one of his musical contemporaries. They are shown here in italics:

---

58. Pontiroli, 188.
59. Milano, Biblioteca Ambrosiana, A 10 Inf.

the Ignorant judge frequently by the Performance, not by the Composition; which caus'd that unparallel'd Master of Musick, my good friend and Maestro *Monteverdi* to vindicate a good Composition ill performed, *to the Duke of Vennice* affirming that had he been Rector Chori, he would have made that Song before judg'd bad, to have pass'd for good. So advantagious and necessary is the Judicious ordering and management of Musick.

In other words, a first-rate director could make a true masterpiece sound absolutely superb. Porter's term "judicious ordering" is echoed by Monteverdi's phrase "mettere all'ordine" in a letter referring to a cantata in honour of the Doge in 1618.[60] It was this process of setting things in order at rehearsal that prepared the way for a convincing performance. This would surely have featured a natural approach to meter, based not on a 4/4 pattern but on a flowing effect, allowing syllable stresses to make their natural effect.

CHIAVETTE OFF-KEY?

Arguments about the role of "chiavette"—the so-called "transposing clefs"—began in the nineteenth century, launched by Kiesewetter and Bellermann. Discussion continued at a later date in articles by Ehrmann, Kroyer, Mendel, Federhofer, Hermelink, and others. English, French and Italian writers followed at a discreet distance. A careful analysis of this literature reveals two features: a tendency to misunderstand what previous contributors had written, and a willingness to heap Pelion upon Ossa. Although I have no wish to interfere with this leisurely quarrel of the musicological gods, I nevertheless venture to make the following observations.

Since the term is Italian and the composers—whose works are supposedly affected—rank either as Italian (Palestrina, Monteverdi) or of comparable affinity (Victoria, Lassus), it has been assumed that their music can be transposed, absolutely at will and without any agreed method, up or down to any key or pitch.

Notorious modern examples on record include the transposition of an entire opera up a whole tone, putting a Magnificat down a fourth, or pushing the bass part of a three-part madrigal up an octave.

---

60. Letter no. 29, 21 April 1618.

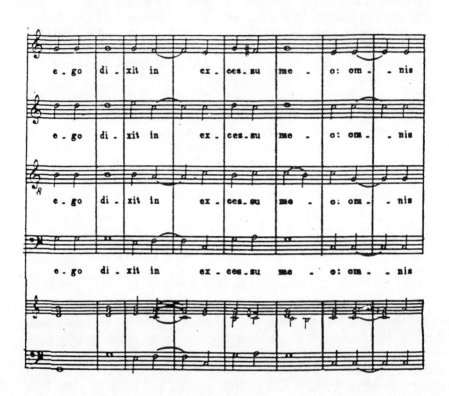

A passage from the psalm *Credidi* in the 1940 edition and in the 1999 edition

This would be comparatively easy to accept if only the early the-
orists, contemporaneous with the composers mentioned, had inves-
tigated this "Frage" with some thoroughness. But if one carefully
scrutinizes the published works of Artusi, Bottrigari, Giustiniani,
Vicentino and Zarlino, it soon becomes clear that they ask no questions of the chiavette and expect no answers.

Nor is there any mention of a "chiavette-problem" in the writings
of Thomas Morley or Marin Mersenne. They recognized "chiavi
naturali" and "chiavi trasportati" (the latter term meaning higher
or lower positions on the staff), but if transposition might sometimes be implied, it was never mandatory.

The sole purpose of the "chiavi trasportati" was to allow the
composer to accommodate all the notes of a voice-part on a simple
stave *without* the use of ledger lines.

Composers did not like ledger lines.
Copyists did not like ledger lines.
Printers did not like ledger lines.
Singers and instrumentalists did not like ledger lines.

All these people would go to immense lengths to avoid having to
interpret parts that frequently went out of range. A universally accepted method of coping with the matter was to move the clef up or
down a third, or move from bass clef to tenor clef in the case of
continuo parts.

In other words, if the "chiavi" were "trasportati," there was
never a question of "musica trasportata." *The clefs were transposed, not the music.* Within the body of a part, the change would
be one of "chiave"; but if it occurred at the beginning, the term
"chiavetta" was employed. Even the most erudite of modern inter-
preters cannot resolve the question of a methodical transposition
pattern based on chiavette. Some say they imply movement a third
up, some say a third down. Others say a fourth or a fifth, up or
down. There is no method in this madness.

There is, indeed, no correlation between chiavette and pitch, because in unaccompanied music pitch depended on the human con-
tent of each choir and the kind of voices selected for any given
performance. The director's business was to know, or discover, the
lowest effective note singable by his bass section, and his next task,
as Ganassi explains, was to look through the bass part in its entirety
and find the lowest note.

With this aligned to the lowest singable note, pitch matters were settled and the rehearsal could proceed. The dialogue *Que dis-tu, que fais-tu, pensive tourterelle?* by Lassus is sometimes cited as an example of chiavette, which do indeed appear in the higher of the two choirs since Lassus takes care to distinguish between the words of the Passer-by and those of the Turtle-dove. This dialogue, like Palestrina's double-choir *Stabat Mater,* can be comfortably and effectively sung by giving the starting pitch a tone lower. Similar small adjustments ensure that each voice-part can be sung without straining up or down.

In the case of works for voices and orchestra, transportation was achieved by using the organ as a transposing instrument. Many of the larger churches deployed high- and low-pitched organs in the centuries spanned by Monteverdi, and much later it was common to accommodate orchestral works by transposing the organ part. William Boyce's *Concerto grosso in D minor* has, among the set of parts in the Bodleian Library, Oxford, an organ part in C minor. This solution may have been adopted at Cremona Cathedral in 1583.

Monteverdi's Mass *In illo tempore,* for six voices, demands downward transposition not because of its chiavette, but by reason of the voice-ranges which on modern staves consistently float into the stratosphere. What looks like a tortuously high-pitched SSATTBar composition comes into line perfectly when the lowest note of the bass part (G) is taken as low F, which yields an ensemble of boys, tenors, and bass-baritones. It was the rich, creamy sound of this ensemble that won Monteverdi his contract at S. Marco.

The Magnificat of his 1610 *Vespers* does not however call for transposition, since all the voice-parts are viable and the highest note of the violins is D, which appears in Riccardo Rognoni's *Selva di varii passaggi* of 1620—no difficult matter for such violin virtuosi as the Rubini brothers from Casal Monferrato. Once again, the only special equipment required would be a low-pitch organ, which would provide a level one tone below standard pitch today.

Similar situations arise in English music, like John Taverner's motet *O splendor patris,* which is prefaced by clefs that clearly have no relation to the pitch as used in performance. With Tallis on the other hand an exquisite set of Lamentations lay in obscurity for centuries while editions topped by sopranos were frequently being used, despite the well-known recommendation of the Bergamasque Pietro Cerone. According to his *El melopeo y maestro* (1613), it was desirable to perform the Lamentations with heavy, deep voices, singing one to a part.

The correct sung pitch is therefore of the greatest importance. I may say that for forty years I have performed, broadcast, or recorded over one hundred works by Monteverdi without feeling the need to transpose anything. His magnificent bass solo *Ab aeterno ordinata sum,* in the *Selva morale,* demands a range from C below the bass staff to F above it; and it is roughly the same range as Handel's bass part in the cantata *Nell'Africane selve* and the Baron Ochs role in Richard Strauss's *Der Rosenkavalier.*

Apart from a few exceptional voices, the human tessitura has not changed very much over the centuries, and the only transposition needed in general is Borodin's—from the piano to the writing desk. Perhaps we should bear in mind the misfortune that occurred during Michael Balfe's early career in Bergamo. On finding his part in the opera too low, he complained to the manager that the orchestra was "troppo basso". The manager promised that all would be well in the evening, but when Balfe arrived at the theatre he found that carpenters had raised the orchestra level by half a metre.[61]

BASSO CONTINUO—BASSO SEGUENTE

Monteverdi calls his bassus part-book a "Basso Continuo"; nevertheless, its music provides a basis for harmonic support either as a basso continuo or as a basso seguente. The first term allows the organist—whether playing on a larger fixed or smaller movable instrument—to accompany few or many voices in a quasi-improvisatory manner. His voice of stops and texture would always be subject to the meaning of the text, as Agazzari emphasizes:

> the chords and the harmony as a whole are subject to and subordinate to the words.
> . . . wherever there are words, there is need of suitable harmony.

By allowing his imagination to be prompted by the basso continuo, he can avoid making numerous scores and creating a library larger than that of a Doctor of Laws. He recommends a different way of

---

61. Morton Latham, *Alfredo Piatti* (London: W. E. Hill, 1901), 24.

playing accompaniments for (a) large choirs and (b) small groups
of one or a few soloists:

> an instrument that serves as a foundation must be played with great care
> and due regard to the size of the choir, because if there are many voices
> it is suitable to play full harmonies; but if there are few, reduce the
> sound and play fewer chords, interpreting the music as purely and accu-
> rately as possible, making no runs or divisions.[62]

The second term—basso seguente—was never used as a part-
book designation but developed a special meaning in rehearsals.
The melodic line would always follow the lowest voice (vocal or
instrumental), whether soprano, alto, tenor, or bass. After the early
years of the seventeenth century the basso seguente (as a musical
term) dropped out of use. But the device itself continued as a simple
scheme "for accompaniment only." Monteverdi's friend and colleague Adriano Banchieri described this technique with admirable
clarity, indicating that nothing whatever should be added to the bass
part. It would become, like Handel's "tasto solo," merely another
color in the ensemble:

> The Author to the Reader:
>   These ecclesiastical symphonies, or French chansons: if you wish to
> play them with all four parts on a keyboard instrument you can score
> them and intabulate them, and this will succeed very well. But if you
> wish to perform them with voices and instruments, let the Organist be
> advised to promote them by playing the Basso Seguente without any
> alteration, but with seriousness and steadiness; and I should not omit to
> tell you regarding this, that in a few days Signor Agostino Agazzari, a
> most renowned musician and organist, will bring out a treatise—a use-
> ful work for concert-givers, and necessary for whoever desires to realize
> the Basso Continuo clearly.[63]

Monteverdi, Agazzari and Banchieri were of like mind on this
one important point: that an organist with an ear for text, topic and
harmony would need no written-out continuo parts. In most of the
Selva repertory a single bass line suffices. Only in *Ab aeterno ordinata sum*, the *Salve Regina* with echo tenor, and the *Pianto della
Madonna* is there need to print the vocal part and continuo in quasi-

---

62. Agostino Agazzari, *Del suonare sopra'l Basso* (Siena: Domenico Falcini,
1607).
    63. Adriano Banchieri, *Ecclesiastiche Sinfonie* (Venezia: Amadino, 1607).

score. The early Mass has no accidentals at all, while the psalms, hymns and motets show only occasional accidentals. These could be cues for the player of the positive organ at rehearsals. In actual performance this kind of support (like the bassoonist who gave the pitch) would become superfluous. The bass line could then be taken by trombone or contrabass.

In Monteverdi's day the trombone, properly played, could be a fairly quiet instrument, blending easily with tenors and basses of the chorus. Luigi Zenobi, a cornettist and singer writing about the year 1601, possibly to Prince Carlo Gesualdo, stresses the need for trombones with a smooth sound:

> These characteristics of the Trombone are revealed in just intonation, in delicate playing, in avoiding the bovine, and in imitating the bass voice.[64]

He emphasizes the need to "avoid the bovine," because a coarse-sounding trombone player could easily ruin the balance of a chamber ensemble, which Monteverdi often had to consider in preparing his music for the private oratory of the Doge or the house parties of royalty and nobility spending time in Venice.

As for the double bass, it was an important instrument in the orchestra of the basilica for centuries. In 1781 the eighteen-year-old Domenico Dragonetti was appointed, and it was to S. Marco that he bequeathed his instrument after his death. A plentiful supply of *violone* players characterized Monteverdi's years in Venice, for they were constantly needed to play basso continuo parts—in other words, to supply 16-foot tone for the small chamber organs, usually *all'ottava* and therefore needing a gamba and double bass to give tonal depth to the ensemble.

Although the director of music often discusses singers in his letters, he hardly ever refers to instrumentalists. There is however one letter which offers a closer look at his musicians, and that is his complaint to the Procurators about the insults hurled at him by Aldegati on June 8, 1637. His musicians were being paid fees for their part in the music at the translation of the body of St. John of Alexandria, which took place on May 17 in the nunnery of S. Daniele.

---

64. Luigi Zenobi, letter to an unnamed prince, Rome, Biblioteca Vallicelliana, R 45 f. 202v; cited in Bonnie J. Blackburn and Edward E. Lowinsky, "Luigi Zenobi and His Letter on the Perfect Musician," *Studi Musicali* 22 (1993): 61–114.

The fees, which took three weeks to arrive, apparently did not give satisfaction to Aldegati. Monteverdi names the others, who apparently had no quarrel with the arrangements:

Sig. Giovanni Battista, called the Bolognese singer of the chapel.
Sig. Gasparo Zorina, a Brescian, who plays the double bass.
Sig. Alovisi Lipomani.
Sig. Don Annibale, a Roman, singer of the chapel.
Sig. Giovanni Battista, the Paduan, who plays trombones.[65]

Of the five musicians named, two were singers and three instrumentalists. Alvise Lipomani and Gasparo Serena, both *violone* players, had joined the orchestra shortly before the event. G. B. Padovan joined in 1624 and remained long after the composer's death. Perhaps it is not without significance that an arbitrary gathering of musicians included three who would have sustained the bass part, for their support of the organ and voices would have counted for much in the acoustics of S. Daniele.

ORGANS AND ORGANISTS

There is no way of counting how many organists worked with Monteverdi during the sixty-five years of his musical life. He must have experienced—as we all have—the good, the competent, and the poor. Passing over his years in Cremona and Mantua, it is clear from his Venetian period that organists playing for him ranged from the merely average executant to players so brilliant as to threaten the effect he was striving for. Although one finds the name of an occasional lutenist or theorbo player among the lists of musicians at S. Marco, their role was largely decorative; and their sound, being evanescent like those of other plucked strings such as the harpsichord, contributed *Augenmusik* and a helpful *ictus,* but very little in the way of foundation tone.

Monteverdi gives us but one glimpse of his heartfelt wishes in the matter of tone and color in organ accompaniments, which can be seen in his discussion of the brilliant Friday evening concerts given in the Hall of Mirrors in the Gonzaga Palace at Mantua. Yet I

---

65. Letter no. 126: 9 June 1637.

have never heard the combination of *organo di legno* and theorbos, which must sound enchanting:

> On a similar splendid occasion I shall have the theorbos played by the musicians from Casale, to the accompaniment of the wooden organ, which is extremely suave, and in this way Signora Adriana and Don Giovanni Battista will sing the extremely beautiful madrigal "Ahi, che morire mi sento" and the other madrigal to the organ alone.[66]

Here is Monteverdi himself telling us of two ways to accompany a duet or a madrigal—either with organ alone, or with organ and plucked string instruments. When he auditioned a male alto at Mantua in the previous year, he tested him not with a lute or theorbo, but with an organ accompaniment:

> I took him straightaway into S. Pietro and had him sing a motet in the organ-loft, and I heard a fine voice, powerful and sustained, and when he sings on the stage he will make himself heard in every corner, well and without strain.[67]

This point in favour of the organ had already been made by Luigi Zenobi, in his letter concerning the perfect musician:

> In solo performance one cannot judge the quality of the bass when he is accompanied by a lute, or a harpsichord, or similar instruments, for instruments of that kind have hardly sounded the note before it vanishes; and thus the bass as well as any other part can make an infinite number of mistakes that pass unnoticed because the vanishing harmony of the imperfect instrument does not let them be heard, except that the connoisseur recognizes them as errors and misunderstandings, and consequently causes the singer to be held ignorant. But it is in singing with the organ where one can judge easily who sings and plays with good taste and with art, if the listener pays careful attention. And this is what betrays the ignorance and presumption of many who, singing in the most deplorable manner to the accompaniment of the organ, thrive on the judgment of the populace and the rabble, who, as soon as they hear a miserable charlatan with a bit of a dog's voice or an asinine disposition, immediately begin to exclaim: "How marvelous, how fine! What a divine voice! What do you think, Mr Dimwit? What do you say, Sir Mumble-Tongue? Is it not miraculous, Sir Bibble-Babble?" And thus many

---

66. Letter no. 11, 22 January 1611.
67. Letter no. 9, 9 June 1610.

wretched birds are scorned by connoisseurs and praised by ignoramuses like them.[68]

The use of organs—two or more of them—in Monteverdi's church music is not a matter of opinion: it is an established fact. Yet performances are still given with only one, or none at all. If modern practitioners can all find and read musicological material, they do not always seem to understand it. They can certainly plead financial or logistical reasons for ignoring the information supplied, and they are entitled to ignore it. But if they do so, they cannot claim the smallest degree of authenticity.

Sansovino's exhaustive account of Venetian churches lists them by *sestiero,* and when the total is reached we find that 144 organs can be found in 121 churches. Thomas Coryate, writing in the early years of the seventeenth century, counted 143 organs, which is close enough to claim that many instruments did indeed exist and were constantly put to good use. Visitors to the city wrote about them with sufficient enthusiasm to establish their central role in music-making, just as in Vivaldi's case a century later.

The difference between the number of churches and the number of organs can probably be explained by the fact that portable instruments were often stored in churches, where there would hardly be a charge for an instrument that might one day be of use in celebrations of a major feast-day. The archives are full of references to the moving of organs back and forth, so that even a partial list of such organological tranpositions would faintly resemble the account-book of a modern furniture-removal corporation.

This superfluity of organs came about because of a growing interest in polychoral music not only in Venice but also in Rome, where certain large-scale events could bring as many as ten choirs and ten organs into action, as is shown in the description by André Maugars of elaborate music for the Feast of St. Dominic at S. Maria sopra Minerva on August 4, 1639:

To enable you to understand this distribution better, I will give you an example by describing to you the most celebrated and most excellent concert that I heard at Rome the eve and the day of St. Dominic at the church of the *Minerva* [S. Maria sopra Minerva]. This church is rather long and wide, and there are two large elevated organs, one on each side

---

68. Zenobi, 99.

of the main altar, where they had also placed two choirs. Along the nave there were eight other choirs, four on one side and four on the other, raised on platforms eight or nine feet high, an equal distance from one another and all facing one another.

With each choir there was a portative organ, as is the custom. You must not be astonished, because one can find more than two hundred [organs] in Rome, while in Paris one could scarcely find two of the same tuning. The leading conductor beat the measure for the main choir, accompanied by the best voices.

With each of the others there was a man who did nothing but keep his eyes on the leading conductor, to conform his own beat to the leader's; in this way all the chorus sang in the same time, without dragging. The counterpoint was decorated, full of fine chants, and many agreeable recitatives. Sometimes a high voice in the first choir sang a *récit,* then one of the third, fourth and tenth answered. Sometimes two, three or four voices from the different choirs sang together, sometimes the parts of all the choirs recited, each in turn, in emulation of each other.

Sometimes two choirs contended with each other, then two others answered. Another time three, four and five solo voices sang together, and at the *Gloria Patri* all the choirs joined together. I must admit that I have never been so delighted; but especially in the Hymn and in the Prose, where ordinarily the conductor tries to do better, I heard singing that was perfectly beautiful: very elegant variety, very excellent inventions, and delightful different movements.[69]

Notwithstanding the clarity and logic of this description, it has been boldly misinterpreted as "proof" that the choirs were singing with only one voice to a part; but since a ten-choir ensemble would call for at least fifty to sixty singers, this "proof" can be dismissed as extremely unlikely.[70] The occasion so vividly evoked by Maugars was a liturgical service at which the two main organs could have been played by Girolamo Frescobaldi and his then pupil, Johann Jacob Froberger. The music was probably by Antonio Maria Abbatini, who composed Masses and motets for groups of up to twelve choirs.

Even though we have no comparable descriptions of services in

69. Maugars, *Response faite à un curieux sur le Sentiment da la Musique d'Italie, Ecrite à Rome le premier Octobre 1639.* Translation after Carol MacClintock, *Readings in the History of Music in Performance* (Bloomington and London: Indiana University Press, 1979), 118.

70. G. Dixon, "The Performance of Palestrina," *Early Music* 22 (November 1994): 669.

Venice during Monteverdi's time, there are letters mentioning vocal and instrumental Vespers within four years of his death, and drawing on the help of his best pupils. The letters are by Paul Hainlein, who travelled from Nuremberg to Venice in 1647, aiming to further his studies and hear as much music as possible. He emphasizes the role of positive organs in Vespers at SS. Giovanni e Paolo on the Feast of the Rosary (October 5–6), and at S. Francesco della Vigna on the Feast of the Conception (December 7–8). The music at SS. Giovanni e Paolo, he says,

> took place last Saturday after the evening hour on the Feast of Our Lady's Rosary and lasted until 3 hours at night [9 P.M.].
> The church is hung with beautiful paintings and tapestries, and in addition a platform was set up within the choir on which the musicians with the 4 positives were placed. At first the organists preluded one after the other, and after this the psalms began, *Dixit Dominus* being the first.[71]

At S. Francesco he heard Cavalli play one of the organs:

> As far as music is concerned, I heard some last Saturday . . . that was performed at the Feast of the Conception of Our Lady [December 8], when a platform was set up. The musicians placed on it consisted of 3 discant singers, 3 altos, 3 tenors and 3 basses, also 4 violins, 2 viole da brazzo, 4 trombones, in ripieno 10 persons, 3 positive organs among which Signor Cavalli played.[72]

THE ORCHESTRA AT S. MARCO

Anybody who wished to assemble a first-rate orchestra in the early seventeenth century had to begin with an outstanding concertmaster—in Venetian terms a *maestro de' concerti*. When Monteverdi arrived in Venice, the instrumentalists were led by a virtuoso cornettist, Giovanni Bassano, who was justly famed for his publications. The *Ricercate, Passaggi et Cadentie* of 1585 had long been regarded as a reliable source-book for the embellishment of wind

---

71. W. Gurlitt, "Ein Briefwechsel zwischen Paul Hainlein und L. Friedrich Behaim aus den Jahren 1647–48," *Sammelbände der Internationalen Musikgesellschaft* 14 (1912–13) 481–99.
72. Ibid.

and string music, while the other—his *Motetti, Madrigali, et Canzoni Francese*—provided a collection of ornamented compositions for general use. The one surviving exemplar was fortunately copied out and left in a safe place by Friedrich Chrysander long before the destruction of the original during World War II.[73]

Bassano continued as head of the instrumental group until 1617, when the position was given to Francesco Bonfante, an altogether different kind of musician. Although he never published anything, his excellence as a leading violinist is attested to by regular increases in pay until his retirement in 1661, by which time he had given some fifty-seven years of service. He and Monteverdi were ably assisted by rank-and-file violinists who have since become famous in other ways, notably Biagio Marini, Antonio Zanetta, Giacomo Rovetta, and Giovanni Battista Fabris. Extra players, including exponents of other stringed instruments, could readily be hired for special feasts.

It is not surprising to find Monteverdi's basic string texture reflected in the lists of players, which reveal a treble-bass penchant encouraged by the hiring of many violins and a few basses, usually noted as *violone* (Giovanni de Ventura) or *violone contrabasso* (his son Giovanni Marchetti). One also finds many cornetto and trombone players, the occasional bassoon—often played by a trombonist—and a sprinkling of theorbos. As printed editions indicate, however, the theorbo was primarily a chamber music instrument, and in larger ensembles an alternative choice to the *violone* or organ. The viola seems to appear in its own right only towards the end of Monteverdi's tenure.[74]

The sound of the violins would have been far more strident than the classical instruments of the later seventeenth century, for favorite makers prior to 1650 were Ventura de Francesco Linarolo, who worked first in Venice and later in Padua, and Andrea Amati in Cremona. The Brescian luthiers were also admired, especially Gaspar da Salò and Giovanni Paolo Maggini. These makers all cultivated a penetrating tone that would set the new instruments apart from the older viols. As for the mixing of instrumental groups, we

73. Hamburg, Staats- und Universitätsbibliothek: Chrysander-Nachlass. See Ernst T. Ferand, "Die Motetti, Madrigali, et Canzoni Francese . . . ," in *Festschrift Helmuth Osthoff* (Tutzing: 1961), 75.

74. Eleanor Selfridge-Field, *Venetian Instrumental Music from Gabrieli to Vivaldi* (Oxford: 1975), 298.

can be certain that this was generally achieved in accordance with Ercole Bottrigari's recommendations in *Il Desiderio,* published in Venice in 1594 and later in Bologna and Milan.

For some unexplained reason the origins of this discussion have been misunderstood in certain literature pertaining to Monteverdi, and it has even been suggested that the "celestial harmony" mentioned in the opening pages by Gratioso Desiderio (Bottrigari) refers to the perfect orchestra for *intermedii* and, by association, for operas.[75] In actual fact, Bottrigari had just attended a concert of vocal and instrumental music given by some forty musicians at the Accademia de Filarmonici in Bologna:

> Having gone a number of times to hear various and diverse musical concerts by voices accompanied by different instruments, I have never experienced the great pleasure that I had imagined and supposed, and which in fact I had hoped to experience. And today particularly, when I attended this one, such was the case; because, having seen a great apparatus of different kinds of instruments—among them a large harpsichord and a large spinet, three lutes of various forms, a great number of viols and a similar large group of trombones, two little rebecs and as many large flutes, straight and traverse, a large double harp and a lyre, all for accompanying many good voices—there where I thought I would hear a celestial harmony, I heard confusion rather than the contrary, accompanied by a discordance, that has offended me rather than given me pleasure.[76]

The sounds emitted by this varied instrumentarium gave Bottrigari pain rather than pleasure, and the expected "celestial harmony" turned out to be utter discord. Bottrigari's theory is that the Philharmonic concert featured too many instruments of unrelated types that were impossible to tune together. But within the self-imposed limitations of the ensemble at S. Marco, the music was bound to be more pleasing to the ear; and in the hands of a good *maestro de' concerti* the use of "ogni sorte de stromenti" referred to in descriptions of festivals at the basilica could indeed result in heavenly harmony. A composer known to Monteverdi and working along

---

75. Philip Pickett, " 'Armonia Celeste': Orchestral Colour and Symbolism in Monteverdi's L'Orfeo," in *Performing Practice in Monteverdi's Music* (Cremona: 1995), 143.

76. Ercole Bottrigari, *Il Desiderio* (Venice: 1594), 3. Translated by Carol MacClintock in *Musicological Studies and Documents* 9 (1962): 13.

similar lines was Giovanni Valentini at the Habsburg court in Vienna in 1637:

> Meanwhile they began to play every sort of musical instrument and to sing *Te Deum laudamus,* which along with the mass and motet were new works by Signor Giovanni Valentini, His Majesty the Emperor's director of music.[77]

The effective combining of instruments with organ, familiar enough in Venice by the late sixteenth century, was certainly known also to the youthful Monteverdi in Cremona. He was twelve years old when his teacher Ingegneri published his Second Book of Madrigals in 1579, and could have taken part in performances at the Accademia degli Animosi. Even more important, he could have played in the two instrumental pieces included in the same books: two *Arie di Canzon Francese* on the first and the eighth tone, intended for a four-part string group.

The cathedral account books provide us with information about occasional but innovative concerts given at Christmas and Epiphany, payment being approved on January 31, 1579:

> At Christmas time he gave various concerts that especially pleased the nobles who came there in great numbers, and all the people. He worked very hard, and for this Marco Antonio Ingegneri received, over and above his salary as a singer, 50 imperial lire, half given at once and the other half allocated for the Feast of the Assumption of the Virgin.[78]

Ingegneri's long-term concert plans revived the long-debated matter of improvements to the existing cathedral organ that had been built in 1480 by Lorenzo Antonio da Bologna.[79] Ingegneri found that the organ pitch was too high to agree with a string ensemble such as one would expect to find in a city where Amati's violins had become famous far and wide. Documents make it clear that the organist Francesco Mainerio and Ingegneri as director of music would become responsible for this major adjustment:

77. Steven Saunders, "The Hapsburg Court of Ferdinand II . . . ," *Journal of the American Musicological Society* 44 (1991): 382.

78. *Liber provisionum* (Archivio della Fabbriceria della Cattedrale di Cremona), 13 July, 1579.

79. Raffaello Monterosso, *Una firma autografa di Marco Antonio Ingegneri in un documento inedito* (Cremona: 1946).

> Let Francesco Mainerio be obliged to lower the pitch of the cathedral organ by about one semitone, so that the pitch of this organ may conveniently correspond to the choir and to the concerts which are given there, and which will continue to be given with all kinds of musical instruments, so that the said music and concerts will unite in the praise of Signor Mainerio, organist of the cathedral, and Signor Marco Antonio Ingegneri, director of music in that same church.[80]

Experts were called in from other cities, memoranda were written, and debates took place. At first it seemed as though Ingegneri would achieve his aim to make life a little less hazardous for his string players, who were beginning to tire of tuning up their strings to breaking point.

The idea became a civic affair. No longer was it a question of convenience for the musicians, for the townspeople thought that some damage might be done to the tonal qualities, and eventually after considerable expenditure and work it was decided to repair the organ but leave it at its former pitch:

> It is better to preserve the liveliness of the sound of this instrument to the content of the city, than to lower it just to suit the musicians; so much the more because those same musicians made the lowering simply for their own benefit.[81]

Monteverdi was thus forewarned of possible problems in the marriage of string polyphony and organ continuo long before he reached Venice, and through Venice a wider world that is still winning him friends and admirers. These, together with witnesses of the revival of his music since the mid-1930s, will see a slow but steady return to the principles that guided him in his life's work. These principles, in no way related to the fads and fashions in performance that come and go in the natural process of growth and decay, are founded on the firm rock of knowledge, which alone can vouchsafe our true understanding of his legacy and our ability to pass it on.

---

80. Archivio di Stato di Cremona, *Archivio Notarile,* not. Livio Beliselli, fil. 2912, f. 337.

81. *Liber provisionum,* 30 July 1583.

3
Claudio! Audio?

DO I HEAR YOU? *Do I read you? asks the modern Monteverdian. Sadly, in many cases the message is far from clear, due to the lack of straightforward and uncomplicated advice on how to perform church music, madrigals and operas by Monteverdi and his contemporaries. This chapter sums up the matter. It assumes, however, that you have an infinitely expanding budget and a sound idea of how to spend it.*

If church music, conjure up a situation involving many professional singers (and some amateurs) with strong voices. You aim to fill the building with sound. The same is true of instruments. In Monteverdi's orchestra the violins were made by Antonio and Girolamo Amati, Gaspar da Salò, Ventura Linarolo, and the young Maggini. They were powerful instruments—not yielding the usual "early instrument" sound, but the kind of sonority that would make a strong impression on a listener in S. Marco.

If voices and instruments are too loud, they can be persuaded to play quietly. But if they are soft and ineffective to begin with, they cannot become louder at the drop of a music stand. The continuo instruments must also be powerful: a gravicembalo (large harpsichord with a 16-foot stop) and not merely a cembalo or harpsichord of the chamber-music type. The same is true of organs, as with the famous concert in S. Marco for the Japanese ambassadors in 1585, when a portable organ was added so that "the two gallery organs and other instruments would make the harmony more magnificent." No lutes or guitars, please!

*   *   *

Monteverdi himself gives most of the necessary information in his letters and prefaces. For the collected letters, see the Italian edition by Eva Lax (Olschki, Florence, 1995) or my English edition (Faber, 1980) or the revised volume published by Clarendon Press, Oxford, in 1995. Page references to the English versions in this chapter will show two numbers, the first for 1980 and the second for 1995. As regards the prefaces,[1] only one reference is necessary here: to the last four words of "Claudio Monteverde à chi legge" in his eighth book, 1638: "*Inve[n]tis facile est ad[d]ere*" [It's easy to add to things discovered]. For example, if you find a ballet apparently scored for two violins and basso continuo, (your knowledge of musical history being sound), then add two viola parts.[2] Similarly with church music, such as a *Dixit Dominus* whose rubric demands four viole da braccio or four trombones, or with a *Sonata sopra Sancta Maria* scored for an obviously lop-sided combination of five wind and three strings.[3] Busy composers rarely wrote out filler parts for violas. Even as late as Lully and Gluck, such lacunae were filled by secretaries or music assistants. Monteverdi usually had an assistant, and knew that other directors of music would be similarly endowed.[4]

The same was true in the world of opera and intermezzo. Even though string strength varied from one orchestra to another, the basic five parts should always be nominally present, just as in a classical orchestra the four-part texture prevailed. For many years it was thought that the dance section in *Il ballo delle ingrate* called for only four parts (and was thus printed in the Malipiero edition), but in 1958 I discovered an additional part in the original edition and was able to restore the texture.[5] The remaining trio sections should almost certainly be similarly fleshed out. A statement that Monteverdi's five-part dance music is much more old-fashioned

---

1. The only nearly complete collection is *Lettere, Dediche e Prefazioni*, edited by Domenico De' Paoli (Rome: 1973).

2. For a reexamination of *De la bellezza le devute lodi* (1607), see my "Monteverdi's Earliest Extant Ballet," *Early Music* 14 (1986): 358–66.

3. Revised edition of the Vespers of 1610 (London: Novello, 1994).

4. Both Cavalli and Rovetta worked with Monteverdi during his time in Venice. Cavalli excelled in playing the organ and composing, whereas Rovetta's talents found their outlet in playing wind and string instruments. In his *Salmi concertati* of 1626, he puns in his preface on "un nuovo vivente Apollo, sovra'l cui verde Monte le vere Muse cercan di ricovrarsi per apprendere i tuoni de gli esquisiti concerti."

5. *Il ballo delle Ingrate* (London: Schott, 1960).

than the four-part texture of the *Combattimento* does not tell the whole story:[6] it was less a matter of fashion than of intent, for the 1608 opera-ballet ranked as a terpsichorean event while the later work of 1624 was a secular oratorio. In other words, both were secular, but one was a dance show while the other had a moralistic tone and required a leaner texture suitable for the percussive reiterations of the *concitato* section.

VIBRATO

Vibrato as an artistic effect can be traced back to very early times, and it was certainly known and practiced in Monteverdi's day. The current verb "ondeggiare" also appears in a hitherto unknown letter of Luigi Zenobi[7] written more than 400 years ago. Telling the alto and tenor singers not to use too much in the way of passage-work, he suggests that they allow the music to rise and fall "gratiosamente ondeggiando" (gracefully vibrating, rising and falling). This effect, known to all string players as well as vocalists, even extended itself to unfamiliar instruments of the cittern family heard by Monteverdi in Mantua.[8]

Zenobi is even more specific when he speaks of the soprano (castrato), consecrating three long paragraphs to its ideal qualities, which must include the freedom to improvise ornaments and develop a non-nasal (boy-like) sound, to avoid excessive bodily movement, to show a mastery of articulated and sedate trills, to cultivate a vibrato (l'ondeggier), and to invent dissonances even when not marked by the composer.[9] Incidentally he casts scorn on the "canto alla francese", with its eye-rolling, chin-trembling, and movement of the upper torso.

There have been excellent studies of vocal technique covering the period from 1575 onwards, with especial reference to Italy, but Zenobi's account is unsurpassed for its insight, its power of description, and its quaint sense of humor. I am certain that in time it

6. Peter Holman, "Monteverdi's String Writing," *Early Music* 21 (1993): 583.

7. Bonnie J. Blackburn and Edward E. Lowinsky, "Luigi Zenobi and his Letter on the Perfect Musician," *Studi musicali* 22 (1993): 61–114, especially 100–101.

8. *Letters,* 416, 427.

9. Blackburn and Lowinsky, 61–114.

will revolutionize vocal study, and much improve the current interpretation of Monteverdi's music, banishing the kind of superficial
snap-judgments which, in the words of a newly-zealous early music
pioneer, are lamentable.[10]

TRANSPOSITION

Nothing in Monteverdi requires transposition. The adoption of a
slightly lower pitch can certainly add to comfort or convenience,
but none of his voice-parts exceeds the normal range. The "Lament
of Arianna" suits a mezzo-soprano or contralto voice perfectly. His
operas can without exception be perfectly cast, while his church
music responds to care and attention by professional voices with a
wide, effective, range. The old tradition outlined by Vincenzo Giustiniani, by which voices capable of singing both bass and tenor,
with a range of many notes, is a case in point, for this singing "alla
bastarda" corresponded exactly with Monteverdi's favourite instrument, the *viola alla bastarda,* which also had a wide range. It might
be said that we need fewer singers but more bastards.[11]

   Those who transpose Monteverdi usually do so not for musical
motives, but for motives of subterfuge whereby an editor's work
can be utilized but not declared as source-material for performance
or recording. Footnotes prove nothing. The advanced string techniques in vogue when Monteverdi lived were sufficient to reach the
half-shift, or third position as it is now called, and international virtuosi such as the Rubini brothers, so often mentioned in his Letters,
were uppermost in his mind when he wrote the Magnificat of the
1610 *Vespers.*[12] Every composer writes for specific virtuosi, as

---

   10. Editorial in *Early Music* 22 (1994): 5.
   11. The illegitimate waifs and strays who were educated at the Venetian
ospedali in the Vivaldi epoch often developed their vocal ranges to an extraordi-
nary extent. In J. C. Maier's *Beschreibung von Venedig* (1789), one finds accounts
of sopranos with a range of three octaves and contraltos able to sing bass parts.
"La Capitona" of the Ospedaletto could be taken for a man, which did not prevent
her subsequent marriage to an aristocrat.
   12. Giovanni Battista and Orazio Rubini, brothers known as "i casaleschi" from
their place of origin, first appear on the list of virtuoso violinists in Mantua in
1597. In 1609, the year before the Vespers publication, Striggio writes to Prince
Francesco about their remarkable performances.

Bach did in his Brandenburg Concertos and Beethoven in his late Quartets. They would have laughed at the idea of downward transposition or simplification of any kind.

The dangers inherent in avoiding the virtuoso bass-baritones whose talents Monteverdi so often drew upon may be judged by the violence done to some of his finest vocal chamber music. One example is the trio, "Parlo, miser, ò taccio?" [Shall I speak or remain silent?].[13] While a mere performance is mercifully forgettable, recordings stay with us for an uncomfortably long time. This unruly piece was recently recorded in such a bizarre manner that instead of hearing the wide-ranging virtuoso bass part probably intended for his friend G. B. Marinoni ("detto Giove"), we are fobbed off with an alto. The entire part, transposed up an octave, willfully changes a texture of SSB to one of SSA, and spoils the colour of the composition as a whole.[14] (See example on page 106.)

One could never get away with this kind of transposition in the Terzetto from act 2 of Mozart's *Figaro* ("Susanna, or via sortite!"), turning the Count into an instant castrato, because opera buffs worldwide would scream with rage and indignation. But apparently with Monteverdi one can transpose down a fifth,[15] up an octave, or (in the case of *Orfeo*) up a tone—and nobody will turn a hair. Nevertheless, I repeat, nothing needs to be transposed.

BALANCE

Monteverdi's settings of Petrarch belong to a very special corner of his life and art. Although "Hor che'l ciel e la terra" looks simple on paper, in fact it requires extremely careful study.[16] He scores it for six voices, two violins, and basso continuo. Not so long ago I heard a performance by a much-touted Monteverdi group whose

---

13. A Guarini setting from Book 7 (1619).

14. See the Letter by Roger Bowers in *The Gramophone* (January 1995), under heading no. 2 regarding music recorded a tone or a minor third too high.

15. It has recently become fashionable to transpose the Magnificat of the 1610 Vespers down so far that the ringing high notes of the solo tenor emerge as a bear-like growl.

16. *Madrigali guerrieri* (Book 8, 1638). For the early Petrarch settings and their relationship to the composer's life, see *Letters,* 50, 43.

Monteverdi: *Parlo, miser, ò taccio?*

Traditore

A passage from *Parlo, miser, ò taccio?* shown in correct and incorrect versions

musicians were individually good, yet the balance sounded poor. Why was this so? First, the six voices were doubled to twelve, despite the fact that any good choral conductor knows that two to a part don't blend. Second, the two baroque violins and gamba were simply inaudible (as were the keyboard instruments), scrubbing away ineffectually while the twelve faithful disciples duly exerted their twenty-four lungs. In the *concitato* section especially ("Guerra è'l mio stato"), bows and fingers could be seen moving frantically. But where was the sound and fury? Towards the end of the sonnet, the word "lunge" is illustrated by a lengthy descending phrase (see page 108).

A passage from *Hor che'l ciel,* **in** *Madrigals, Book 8*

The ending of *Hor che'l ciel*

Its immediate repetition within itself, as well as the fully harmonized restatement, shows that the G-F step should and must be G-F sharp. But in the performance I heard, the F natural hovered awkwardly over E minor. At least one copy of the original edition has a ficta sharp in ink, probably in Monteverdi's hand.

The solution to any balance problem is to accept the composer's advice: adjust the number of instruments to the size of the room. This should be done in all areas—madrigals, ballets, operas, church music. Monteverdi did not write all his music for a touring group whose limited possibilities could be thought to embrace all situations. What's good for *La finta giardiniera* is less satisfactory for *La finta pazza Licori*.

CONTINUO

Only a decade after Luzzaschi published his delicious solos, duets and trios of 1601, Severo Bonini affirmed that musicians only favored little songs with harpsichord accompaniment.[17] Shortly afterwards, when Monteverdi's madrigals began to call for harpsichord continuo, the rules of the Accademia dei Floridi at Bologna guided by his friend Banchieri mentioned the obligatory "concerti di voci alla spinetta" at meetings.[18] Some fifteen years later Vincenzo Giustiniani, recalling the musical gifts of Cardinal Montalto, praised his abilities as a singer and keyboard player.[19] And did not Monteverdi's very first opera call for two "gravicembali"?

When *Orfeo* was broadcast in 1952 from Studio 1 Maida Vale, I saw to it that all the continuo instruments specified by the composer were seen and heard.[20] There were 2 harpsichords, 3 arch-lutes, 2 arch-citterns, 2 positive organs, a regal and a harp—eleven instruments in all, not including viole da gamba and bassi da gamba. Nowadays, although the BBC has an infinitely larger budget, the continuo sections have shrunk to a state of virtual inaudibility, which is to destroy Monteverdi's conception of his own masterpiece. We have more than ample proofs of his fondness for plucked

---

17. *Discorsi e regole sovra la musica,* edited by M. A. Bonino, 100.
18. *Letters,* 211, 214.
19. *Letters,* 234, 239.
20. Broadcast on June 6 and 9, 1952. This performance was the first to bring out the underlying metre in such items as the introductory Sinfonia to act 2 and the hemiolas in "Vi ricorda o boschi ombrosi."

keyboard instruments, and if he lists theorbos in a letter of January 1611, they are there only to supply the ictus to an organ with wooden pipes, "which is extremely suave."[21]

In 1615 he recommends a "spineta arpata" and two small lutes for the ballet *Tirsi e Clori,*[22] and harpsichords also appear in the continuo section of *Le Nozze di Tetide* in 1616.[23] As for the *Combattimento* of 1624, it was accompanied by "cinque viole che continuera con il Clavicembano." At Parma in 1628 he used the claviorganum, which brought together, in one box, a harpsichord and an organ, controlled by one keyboard.[24]

This same event also featured pipe and reed organs. Sabbatini's book, *Pratica di fabricar scene e machine ne' teatri,* published at Ravenna in 1638, stresses the need to design the stage set specifically to accommodate these organs.[25] They formed an important part of Monteverdi's life from his earliest years, for when he began to play stringed instruments in Cremona at the age of 12, the cathedral concerts given by his teacher Ingegneri were imperilled by the high pitch of the organ.[26] The concerts proved so successful, however, that the chapter even considered lowering the pitch of the organ to suit the orchestra.[27]

At twenty-seven, when he played for Vespers in the plains of Hungary before Duke Vincenzo's assembled army, it was obvious that a theorbo would not sound very well in the open air.[28] Leading a male alto into S. Pietro for an audition in 1610, he gave him a motet to sing to the organ.[29] He did not suggest the practice room and a lute. Performing his Mass for an audition in Venice in 1613, he hired two positive organs to help out the main organs. Directing Vespers in 1620 for the Feast of St. John Baptist in S. Giovanni Elemosinario, he was heard by visitors to make use of two organs, one of them still visible today.[30] After his death, a German student

21. *Letters,* 86, 75.
22. *Letters,* 107, 99.
23. *Letters,* 116, 110.
24. *Letters,* 391, 398.
25. Simon Maguire, "The Bumper D. I. Y. Book of Stage Sets," *Opera Now* (July 1991): 60–61.
26. Cremona, Archivio di Stato, Arch. Not. fil. 2912, f.337.
27. Cremona, Archivio della Fabbriceria della Cattedrale, cassetta 5, 25 Nov. 1582.
28. Denis Stevens, "Monteverdiana 1993," *Early Music* 21 (1993): 566.
29. *Letters,* 72, 66.
30. Stevens, "Monteverdiana," 574.

wrote home about Vesper services given in two Venetian churches by pupils of Monteverdi: Cavalli and Rovetta, and in all instances two or three organs were in use.

There is one vital factor that emerges from Monteverdi's correspondence, and that is the need for fully-trained professional voices—as a choir, not as a madrigal group. The singers he used at all his churches were professionals, many with tremendous voices, such as that of Piero Peren, who could fill a building even larger than S. Marco. They consisted of castrato voices, soprano, and alto, with natural tenors and basses. That produced a totally different sound from the present-day youthful choirs of boys (women), counter-tenors, tenors, and basses. These are fine for many purposes, but let not their directors dare to call them "authentic!"

Favourite "authentic" ploys of today include the stiffening of amateur bodies with professionals, or singing with one voice to a part in order to fit in with some shambling shoe-string program budget. All very well in madrigals, but hardly right for the kind of concert reported by the French gamba player André Maugars in his *Response faite à un Curieux sur le Sentiment de la Musique d'Italie,* written in October 1639 as an eye- and ear-witness account of a performance on the Feast of S. Dominic at the Church of S. Maria sopra Minerva in Rome.

Maugars tells us that one could easily find two hundred organs in Rome, and we know that more than one hundred forty were listed in Venice by Sansovino. As for the music itself, even the most casual glance through a catalogue or bibliography reveals that cembalo, lute or theorbo regularly accompanied secular vocal and instrumental music, while organ and basso da gamba supported church music or church sonatas. To the musician of Monteverdi's age the distinction was so clear that there was no point in arguing about it. But in modern recordings, instruments of the lute-type are used increasingly because they save the trouble and expense of hiring and moving harpsichords. All very well, provided one doesn't make a claim for authenticity.

That the harpsichord's noble sounds were widely appreciated is clear from a sentence in Giovanni Battista Doni's *Lyra Barberina,* where he mentions that besides the multiplicity of continuo instruments in Rome and Florence there were "in particular harpsichords of great size," by which he clearly means the "gravicembali" used in such works as Gagliano's *Dafne* and Monteverdi's *Orfeo.*

CONCLUSION

Choral directors who read this and realize that their singers are not loud enough will be even more disappointed when they study what has been said about music of an even earlier period, where refinement of tone and a subtle balance of timbre are needed. Yet it is not all a matter of dynamics, for there is (or should be) a deeper side—the realization in pure sound of a state of mind. Needless transposition is largely occasioned by unenlightened directors who are often, it seems, unaware of what sound their choir should be making. Monteverdi was as sensitive to the needs of S. Marco as he was aware of the scaling-down necessary for the doge's private oratory. Once again it is a question of understanding the implied meaning of the title-page of the 1610 Vespers, a work which grew slowly over a period of some fifteen years (1595–1610). The final test of a performance or a recording is not how slick or glamorous it is, but how truly it realizes the musical thought that dominates the composer's mind. This is open only to those who know the man as well as the music.

4
Acoustics, Tempo, Interpretation

THE CONVERSATIONAL TONE OF *this chapter betrays its origin as the opening address of the International Congress on "Performing Practice in Monteverdi's Music," held at Goldsmith's College, University of London, December 13 and 14, 1993. It coincided with widespread observations of the 350th anniversary of the composer's death.*

The people who could have learned most from those papers did not, of course, turn up, so that standards of interpretation have gone steadily downhill even since the Congress. Although I have made this observation in other publications, it may take quite a few years for matters to improve as dramatically as they should.

It is axiomatic that when there were hardly any scholarly and imaginative individuals to tell us how to perform this music, a chosen few used their instincts and gave interpretations that still inspire us today (Nadia Boulanger); but in a world full of "instant Monteverdi" fiends, who rarely read the right books or articles—and even if they do, might just as well be standing on their heads—there is more deliberate misinterpretation than ever before.

I make no apology for insisting that only three objects are essential for a modern Monteverdi performance: a photo-copying machine, a theorbo, and a microphone. Nothing else whatever is necessary.

*   *   *

Il divino Claudio—as we may well call him in this solemn commemorative year of his death—the divine Claudio never went so far as to claim expertise in the art and science of acoustics, but he was always aware of the profound effect they had on singing and playing, whether in the magnificent churches he served as *maestro di cappella,* or in the opulent palazzi he visited as director of a chamber ensemble; and he would have been the first to recognize and respect the relationship between acoustics and tempo, also to acknowledge and acquiesce in the sovereignty of tempo over interpretation.

A supreme interpreter himself, he was acutely aware of his own worth in this respect, and once said to the doge of Venice (probably Giovanni Bembo, 1615–18), who had been disappointed by some performance in which Monteverdi was not involved: "Had I been able to rehearse and perform that same music, Your Most Serene Highness would have considered as good what he formerly regarded as bad." It was Walter Porter, Monteverdi's only English pupil, who reported that conversation, adding "so advantageous and necessary is the judicious ordering and management of Musick."[1]

We still face the same problems today, in ordering and managing Monteverdi's music and spreading his message around the world. Acoustics, tempo, interpretation. If we solve these problems, his message will enter with ease the minds of listeners, and quit them with difficulty, for it will have made its unforgettable and ineradicable mark. But if we do not solve them, there will be confusion worse confounded. Monteverdi's friend Aquilino Coppini, who made sacred contrafacta of early madrigals, pointed out to Hendrik van den Putten that "the Monteverdi pieces need longer pauses, resting occasionally, allowing retardation, and at times even pressing on. There is in them a wonderful power to move the passions exceedingly."[2] And we know from a sonnet by Muzio Manfredi, who used to attend the musical parties given at the Palazzo del Te, near Mantua, that he was sometimes moved to tears by what he heard; and that the hostess of those parties, who was also a singer, leaned over and offered him her handkerchief. She was Agnese del Carretto, Marchioness of Grana, and Duke Vincenzo's mistress.[3]

She and her fellow-artistes—Adriana Basile, Francesco Rasi, Caterina Martinelli—were all well-acquainted with certain techniques

---

1. *Motets of Two Voyces* (London: 1657). Porter's MS note in the copy at Christ Church Library, Oxford.

2. *Aquilino Coppini in Ticinense Gymnasio Artis Oratoriae Regij Imperatoris Epistolarum Libri sex* (Milan: 1613). Unique copy in Biblioteca Nazionale Braidense, Milano.

3. Iain Fenlon: *Music and Patronage in Sixteenth-Century Mantua* (Cambridge University Press: 1980), 1:149.

of interpretation that are now, unfortunately, almost lost to view. Coppini's advice about tempo is one of them, and the composer's own advice about representative music—whether a madrigal from *Il pastor fido* or the trio "Non avea Febo ancora" from the Eighth Book—that this music "in genere rappresentativo" should follow not the beat of the director's hand, but rather the spirit and meaning of the music, as we experience it in our souls. One might even go back to the elder Alessandro Striggio, who in a letter to the Duke of Tuscany said that the madrigals would go well when they had been memorized and when the words were well enunciated.[4]

There were problems with the acoustics in certain rooms in the Palazzo del Te. The Sala de' Giganti, for instance, allowed a whisper in one corner of the room to be heard with startling clarity in the opposite corner. And we know from Giovanni Battista Doni's treatise *Lyra Barberina* (c. 1640) that one could hear comparable echo effects in the ducal palace itself, where Monteverdi gave concerts every Friday in the Hall of Mirrors.

The echo concept is of course important acoustically, as we know from *Orfeo* and the Vespers of 1610, to give but two examples. The echo idea is also important musically. I recently heard a Radio 3 performance of a duet from Book 7, "Vorrei baciarti, O Filli"— based on a Marini poem that Monteverdi had skilfully split into a vehicle for two countertenors. The performance was lamentable from almost every point of view, but especially because the director had misunderstood the words "a dui contralti." In Monteverdi's day "contralto" meant male alto or, as we would say, counter-tenor. (Remember when in 1610 he asked to audition "un certo contralto venuto da Modena"). Nowadays the term implies a low female voice, so what we heard was two fruity contraltos singing, for some strange reason, "I want to kiss you, Phyllis; I want to kiss you, Phillis." Yet nobody, least of all Marini and Monteverdi, wanted us to think of this as a lesbian madrigal. The musical echo was of course omitted, as indeed was the continuo group favoured by the composer: two theorbos (or archlutes) and an organ with wooden pipes. All we heard was an effete and pointless plunk on the ubiquitous lute, without which no modern performance of any music by Monteverdi seems even remotely possible.

If the continuo cannot be heard, how can the singers manage? It

---

4. Letter of 24 August 1584, cited by Riccardo Gandolfi in 'Lettere inedite,' *Rivista musicale italiana* 20 (1913): 532.

is obviously a question of grappling with unusual acoustical problems, which brings us back to Agnese del Carretto in the Palazzo
del Te, and Adriana Basile and others in the Hall of Mirrors. The
artistes had to calculate their speeds with care and circumspection,
for a tempo suitable for one room would not be right for another.
The ear alone would be the judge. What is more, every musician
and every director of music had to consider the damping effect
brought about by the voluminous court costumes worn at that time
by both men and women. Those costumes would absorb sound,
they would reduce resonance time, and permit a marginally quicker
tempo. So what is the problem nowadays? Simply that when recordings are made, the studio is empty and the performers are wearing modern dress, with the entirely foreseeable result that the clarity
of syllables and words is often lost in the echo—"bombinans in
vacuo," as one might say.

A pity we cannot visualize the scene at the Palazzo Mocenigo,
now the Royal Danieli Hotel, where the première of *Il Combattimento* took place in 1624. Of one thing I am certain: Monteverdi,
with his remarkably sensitive ear, tested out the room well in advance to ensure that the acoustic would project—not absorb—the
hammered syllables like *l'onta irrita lo sdegno alla vendetta alla
vendetta.* He would take no chances, permit no failures.

Continuing with this investigation of venues for music, we should
note that possibly the greatest challenge of all came about at Parma
in 1627, when a new theatre was being constructed in the courtyard
of S. Pietro Martire. Monteverdi was at that time being assisted by
Antonio Goretti, who took the maestro to look at the half-com-
pleted building in October. At first all seemed well; but before the
visit came to an end, Goretti had expressed doubts about the effect
on the acoustic when the roof was added.

By February of 1628 problems had been largely solved, and the
chief architect Francesco Guitti was able to write to the authorities,
"At last Monteverdi has found the right sound-effect, because I
made a place ready for his use and he very much likes it." Much
experimentation was necessary in the placing of musicians, for
there were five orchestras seated in the *cortile da basso,* where the
torneo *Mercurio e Marte* was to take place. Not only had each
group to hear the others clearly, but the audience as a whole had to
be able to take in everything, whether in front of the proscenium,
behind it, or above the entrance doors.

Secular and occasional music, in rooms small and large, brought with it problems that each and every musician had to solve as best he could. In church music, the challenge was if anything greater, since a church must be not only an appropriate sounding-board for sermons, but an effective echo-chamber for music, whether chant or polyphony. The root of this problem of duality, a need to be aware of two acoustical phenomena within one building, is aptly shown by the early sixteenth century Venetian church, S. Francesco della Vigna. Monteverdi is not known to have made music in this church, but he must have been well acquainted with it, for his pupils Rovetta and Cavalli often took part in the music performed there in the last decade of his life.

Amidst great solemnity, its foundation stone was laid in 1534 by the Doge Andrea Gritti. The design was entrusted to Jacopo Sansovino and later on the facade, to Palladio. But owing to differences of opinion about architectural proportions, the doge asked Francesco Giorgi, from the monastery of San Francesco, to advise him.

The monk had published in 1525 a challenging if not controversial work, *De harmonia mundi totius,* which attempted to blend Christian doctrines with neo-Platonic thought, and his main argument was based on the mysterious efficacy of certain numbers and ratios. This advice, summarized for present purposes, shows us what the Doge had to consider:

> I recommend that all the chapels and the choir be vaulted, because the priest's words and music echo better from the vault than they would from the rafters. But in the nave, where there will be sermons, I recommend a ceiling, so that the voice of the preacher may not escape or re-echo from the vaults. I should like to have it coffered with as many squares as possible, because they will be very convenient for preaching: this the experts know, and experience will prove it.[5]

And so we have dual concepts: the priest and his music under the vault, then the preacher and his sermon under the ceiling. Where does the polyphony enter into all this? A description by Paul Hainlein, a young German student in 1647, of Vespers for the Feast of the Conception of the Blessed Virgin, tells us that there were at least 12 singers, another 10 as ripieno, 6 stringed instruments, 4 trombones, and 3 organs—some three dozen musicians altogether.

---

5. Rudolf Wittkower, *Architectural Principles in the Age of Humanism* (London: 1962), 156.

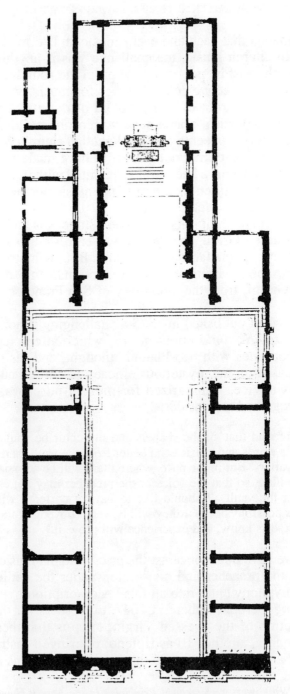

Plan of S. Francesco della Vigna, Venice

One of the organs was played by Francesco Cavalli. A platform (*palco*) was used, and although we have no precise details of placing, there must have been an attempt to separate the solo singers from the ripieno, each group having its separate organ continuo, the third organ being used to accompany the strings and trombones.[6]

Now the widest possible space in which to deploy such a large body effectively would be at the widest point in the church, between two large arches on the left and right.

If you look at the plan of S. Francesco della Vigna, you see clearly the effect of the designs put forward by Giorgi. Relying on Greek harmonic theory and in particular the ideas of Pythagoras, Plato, and Aristotle, he shows that just as there is a harmony in music based on such elementary concepts as 1:2 being an octave, and 2:3 a fifth, so there is a comparable harmony in the proportions of architecture. The church, he says, should have a nave 9 paces wide, and its length 27 paces. The cappella grande at the far end of the nave should be 9 paces long and 6 wide, and these measurements are repeated in the choir behind this chapel. The entire length of the church is therefore 5 times 9. He suggests making the chapels on each side of the nave 3 paces wide, or one-third of the width of the nave. One part of the church is however an extension of this scheme, a 4:3 relationship (diatessaron), which is that of the transept chapels to that of the nave.

There was of course no attempt to apply one art to the other. What mattered was to indicate their close relationship within the all-embracing concept of harmonic proportions. We should also bear in mind the theories of a notable English ambassador to Venice in the early seventeenth century, Sir Henry Wotton, who belonged to the Inigo Jones circle. In his *Elements of Architecture* of 1624, Wotton reminds us that "in truth, a sound piece of good Art, where the Materials being but ordinary Stone, without any garnishment of Sculpture, do yet ravish the beholder (and he knows not how) by a secret Harmony in the Proportions."

In the interaction of space and harmony, it must be admitted that most Renaissance churches enjoy a fine and spacious acoustic, always kind to music as long as there is a gathering of people to soak up some of the sound, and perhaps some of the hangings and pictures mentioned in many contemporaneous accounts of services to absorb even more. A director of music being in many ways con-

---

6. Denis Stevens, "Monteverdiana 1993," *Early Music* 21 (1993): 572.

strained by this acoustical frame, there was an optimum speed at which the text could be clearly heard. We might also consider ornaments, for since these moved faster than the basic structural counterpoint, it was necessary to hear them, too, in their proper context.

Much of course depended on the skill of the singer, and whether he possessed the kind of technique to project the ornamentation. When a young bass arrived in Venice from Bologna in 1627, Monteverdi drew attention to his singing a motet "with a few short runs here and there, and little ornaments, with a decent trillo. The voice is very pleasing but not too deep."[7] At an earlier stage in his career, at Mantua, he had auditioned a visiting counter-tenor from Modena, who had to sing a motet in the cathedral. "I heard a fine voice," wrote Monteverdi, "powerful and sustained, and when he sings on the choir-steps he can make himself heard in every corner very well, and without strain."[8]

As research into Monteverdi's life proceeds, we find his name associated with more and more churches, not only in Cremona, Mantua, and Venice, but also in Milan, Bologna, and Rome. If his Venetian connections still remain the best-known and most numerous, we must remember that here too we begin to see more topographical material coming to light, for example in the early journals and letters of the composer-diplomat Constantijn Huygens. Visiting Venice with friends in 1620, he went with them to the church of S. Giovanni del Rialto, so called for its proximity to the Rialto Bridge. It was more properly termed S. Giovanni Elemosinario—St. John the Almsgiver; this name derived from the fact that, on the death of his wife and children, Giovanni had given all his possessions to the poor, and became a priest. In the latter part of his life, in the year 610, he was made Patriarch of Alexandria, and was especially looked up to by the Venetians.

When Huygens and his friends arrived, they found themselves at the beginning of a vesper service in honor of an even more eminent holy man, St. John the Baptist, and with some excitement Huygens noted in his diary that on June 24, 1620, they had the enormous pleasure of hearing Monteverdi conduct his own compositions. There were 10 or 12 voices, and an instrumental group conprising 4 theorbos, 2 cornetts, 2 bassoons, 2 violins, a huge basso da

7. Letter of 13 June 1627 (No. 97). Denis Stevens, *The Letters of Claudio Monteverdi* (Oxford: Clarendon Press, 1995).

8. Letter of 9 June 1610 (No. 9). *Ibid.*

gamba, and organs, all played with great expertise and panache.[9] Since the church still exists, it would not be difficult to reconstruct the event, following those clues as to orchestral and vocal forces. It has, by the way, already been recorded, the only sad omission being the motet that Monteverdi composed for the day, "Fuge anima mea, fuge mundum," published in the same year, in Lorenzo Calvo's *Symbolae diversorum musicorum.*

On July 19, 1620, just one month after the vespers in S. Giovanni Elemosinario, Monteverdi informed Striggio of the *andata,* or procession of Doge and Signoria to the church of the Redentore on the Giudecca, on the third Sunday in July.

At Low Mass, with thanksgiving prayers for deliverance from the plague of 1576, the choir of S. Marco and its director sang motets at the Offertory and Elevation. Although the composer does not mention this fact in his letter, Martinioni's additions to Sansovino's *Venetia, città nobilissima* supply the missing information.

Palladio's magnificent structure poses unusual acoustical problems, as may be seen from the outside and from the façade. The interior contains three deep chapels on each side, but no aisles whatsoever; as for the nave, it is clearly detached from the centralized area with its three semi-circular apses. The one behind the altar, formed by a series of free-standing columns, derives from a concept inspired perhaps by the Roman baths, but now transferred to a sacred milieu. As Rudolf Wittkower has remarked, these columns form a crescendo near the altar, they maintain the uniformity of the centralized part, and they invite the eye to wander into the space beyond. That is where the motet choir may have been placed.

Monteverdi's task here was to overcome the fact that his musicians were out of view and at a considerable distance from the assembled congregation of city officials, priests, and worshippers.

No discussion of tempo and acoustic in the context of Monteverdi could leave out his "Sonata sopra Sancta Maria." As with much of his vocal music, this mainly instrumental composition calls for flexibility of tempo allied to an understanding of what happens in the orchestration. In this work, the texture is stated to be for eight instruments, but the fact that one instrumental part is labelled "Trombone ovvero Viuola da Brazzo" points to an attempt to re-

---

9. See J. A. Worp, *Constantijn Huygens, journal van zijne reis naar Venetie in 1620,* «Bijdragen en mededeelingen van het Historisch Genootschap» (The Hague: 1894), 128–29.

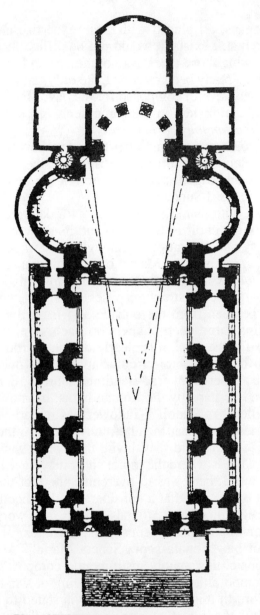

Plan of Il Redentore, Venice

duce to eight parts what should clearly be a ten-part ensemble, the five strings contrasting with five winds. All the other double-choir works in this publication are for evenly matched groups: 4 plus 4, or 5 plus 5.

Accordingly what we have to do is supply the two missing parts in the string group: the two violas—or in Monteverdi's terminology "viole da brazzo." Since music is all in the part-books, nothing new has to be composed. It is simply a case of distribution.

A frequently misinterpreted section is the change of meter at bar 129/130, where the hemiola can only be clarified in modern notation by halving the note-values and using beams for the 6/8 groups. The shift of meter now becomes apparent.

I should mention at this stage that the clue, and indeed cue, for the correct orchestral distribution is the trombone doppio: when he starts to play, it is a sign that the wind band enters.

As a result of all this, the Sonata becomes a work that is more richly scored than was at first suspected, and it should therefore move at a dignified pace. What we hear in so many modern recordings is not so much a beautiful litany that is solemn, but an ugly litter that is a solecism.

A comparable failure to guess what the composer is driving at may be seen in the so-called solo "Nigra sum" in the Vespers, where, in modern concert performances, a well-built and weighty tenor, white, and in white tie, usually steps forward and sings "I am black but shapely" [Nigra sum sed formosa]. But the Song of Songs tells us that these words are sung by the Shulamite maiden, to whom King David soon replies, "Surge, amica mea," indicating that the "motet" is actually a dialogue for two voices, contralto and tenor.

It is not necessary to be a cryptologist to guess at the proper performance of most of Monteverdi's sacred and secular music. Nevertheless, it sometimes helps.

Anyone who has directed a large-scale vocal and instrumental group in S. Marco will know that the tempo usually adopted for the Sonata would be impossible. How then is it done on record? By skillful but dishonest microphone placement, so that "close miking" permits clarity of articulation even at ultra-rapid speeds, no matter what the natural resonance of the building dictates.

Having conducted Monteverdi's music in such edifices as S. Marco, Westminster Abbey, the Jesuitenkirche Luzern, Westminster Cathedral, and (larger than all of these) the Shrine of the Immacu-

(Vespers of 1610, edited by Denis Stevens, London, Novello, 1994)

A passage from *Vespers of 1610*, (1994 edition)

(Vespers of 1610, edited by Denis Stevens, London, Novello, 1994)

Another passage from the same

DB tacet

late Conception in Washington DC, I know that the tempo must take into account the overall acoustic and its reverberation time. We must bear in mind that Monteverdi's orchestral and choral resources were, at any rate in Venice, often quite large, and the continuo section numerous and rich—an essential ingredient which appears to have been lost sight of in recent performances, broadcasts, and recordings.

When the church itself was large, as in the case of S. Marco, or SS. Giovanni e Paolo, where the obsequies of Cosimo II of Tuscany took place on May 25, 1621, Monteverdi's responsibilities grew even greater. He and his musicians were placed behind temporary walls inside the building, as a contemporaneous print shows us: they were in one of the corners in the background. We may have no accurate description of the musical forces on that occasion, but it is possible to reconstruct the liturgy and deduce from it the approximate size of choir and orchestra. For such a great and solemn service, we may be sure that everything was done to produce an effect of maximum dignity and power. Remember, they were not seeking after the quick and trick effects of modern recordings, but rather the kind of sound that would most deeply impress the visiting Florentine dignitaries as much as it moved the native Venetians.

Only three years after Monteverdi's death, his pupil Rovetta directed vespers at SS. Giovanni e Paolo for the Feast of the Rosary on October 5 and 6, 1647. The description of this and other events appeared in Paul Hainlein's letter to his patron in Nuremberg. We hear that thirty-six to forty musicians were present, among them four organists and four trombone-players. Let me sum up by reiterating and stressing the importance of church acoustics in determining the speed of any given performance. And if we evoke Monteverdi again on some future anniversary of his birth or death, let us do so quietly and with due care, bearing in mind the poem by his friend Leonardo Quirini:[10]

> O tu che in nere spoglie
> del gran padre de' ritmi e dei concenti
> l'essequie rinovelli e le mie doglie,
> segui gli uffici tuoi dolenti e mesti,
> ma pian, sì che no 'l desti;

---

10. *Parnaso Italiano: Poesia del Seicento* (Torino: UTET, 1964, 1:890. "In morte di Claudio Monteverdi padre della musica."

ch' egli estinto non è, come tu pensi,
ma stanco dal cantar dà al sonno i sensi.

[O you, clothed in black, who call to mind the funeral rites of the great
father of rhythms and harmonies, and my mourning, perform the sad
and sorrowful offices, but quietly, so that you wake him not; for he has
not left us as you seem to think, but tired of singing gives his senses
over to sleep.]

5

Iconografia Claudiana

UNTIL RECENTLY, COMPARATIVELY FEW *musical scholars interested themselves in iconography. Musicology's main thrust was towards the production of scholarly editions, which succeeding generations contrived to filch photographically, perform, broadcast, and record without so much as a printed acknowledgment of the editors and publishers whose joint sacrifices of time and money had caused it to be reproduced in such abundance. The marble-hearted fiends who thus displayed their ingratitude proved even more furtive than the countless operators a catamini, for their real but unavowed intention was to avoid payment of copyright fees. In this way they have killed the geese that laid so many golden eggs. One may add that these digitalized and computerized musical thieves are precisely the ones who give elaborate credits to choirs, orchestras, recording teams and instruments makers ancient and modern. All these are "in," but musicologists are "out"—at least for the time being.*

This does not happen in iconography, because in general no copyright exists in old paintings and no copyright fee is payable to expert cleaners and restorers. The material is available to anyone armed with a camera. In my earlier days, I would apply to librarians and superintendents for permission to use my SLR, and in that palmy period would be entrusted with portraits or manuscripts worth untold fortunes while I photographed them using a slow-speed colour-accurate film that still yields admirable prints. Nowadays one has to place orders through official and time-consuming channels.

* * *

130

Some examples of this personal photography were included in my article "Musicians in 18th-century Venice" (*Early Music* 20 [1992]: 402–8), which was a purely local parergon to the groundwork for my study of Monteverdi's correspondence. The pictorial source for this article (Museo Correr, Gradenigo 49) also contains a portrait of Monteverdi by the illustrator of this four-volume manuscript, Gian Grevenbroch (Jan van Grevenbroeck, 1737–1807), who as he tells us based it on an oil painting, very probably the one by Bernardo Strozzi, who was active in Venice from 1631 onwards. This likeness was once again brought into service immediately after the composer's death, when the Venetian engraver Giacomo Decini reproduced it in a medallion on the title-page of *Fiori Poetici*.

Strozzi's portrait is referred to in Marco Boschini's poem "La Carta del Navegar Pitoresco," and once formed part of a private gallery belonging to Paolo del Sera, a nobleman from Florence. Boschini, after praising Strozzi's work, draws attention to the sensitive portrayal of Monteverdi's emotions as he listens to the motets or madrigals suggested in a neighboring picture by Giorgione.

> Ghé 'l retrato vesin del Monteverde,
> de man del Strozza, pitor genoese,
> penel che ha fate memorande imprese,
> sí che Fama per lú mai no se perde.

Portraits of Monteverdi by Grevenbroek and Decini

Par giusto che sia là, per ascoltar
quei madrigali aponto e quei moteti.
L'è lá tuto atention. Più vivi afeti
nò se podeva veramente far.

[The neighbouring painting is of Monteverdi by the Genoese artist
Strozzi, whose brush has so limned things to be remembered that Fame
will never forget him. It seems right for him to be there, to hear precisely those madrigals and motets. He is all attention: more sensitive
emotions could not be depicted.]

Strozzi's portrait, probably executed when the composer was in
his mid-sixties, shows us a pensive and serious musician holding an
open part-book, the contents of which are not visible. On leaving
Venice, it somehow found its way to Ireland, later joining the collection of Oskar Strakosch. It is now in the Musikverein, Vienna.
In addition, a copy was sent to Monteverdi's imperial patrons and
has often been reproduced from the Tiroler Landesmuseum Ferdi-
nandeum in Innsbruck.

All three portraits—Grevenbroch, Strozzi I and Strozzi II—show
the composer in his everyday canonicals, implying a date after
April 6, 1632, when he was ordained priest in S. Maria Zobenigo,
also called S. Maria del Giglio. Just a stone's throw from La Fenice,
it was a fit stepping-stone in his career, with its organ panels
painted by Tintoretto and its memorials to the philosopher Sebas-
tiano Foscarini and the poet Hieronimo Molino. Notable too that
some two centuries after the première of the *Combattimento di Tancredi e Clorinda* in the Palazzo Mocenigo on the opposite side of
the Piazza S. Marco, a work on the same subject, Rossini's *Tancredi,* was given for the first time at La Fenice.

Traveling to the diametrically opposed realms of the possible and
the impossible, we turn to the head-and-shoulders of a presumed
Monteverdi when young. This belongs to the collection of Western
Art in the Ashmolean Museum, Oxford. Although its exact provenance is unknown, it may have been a musical lace in the booty
brought back from financially besieged Mantua by Nicholas Lanier,
the English composer, gamba player, and painter who visited the
city in August 1625. How old is the youth holding the viola bastarda, if that is what it purports to be? If about twenty-three, he
could just have arrived in Mantua; if twenty and celebrating the
publication of his *First Book of Madrigals,* he would still be in

Portrait of Monteverdi by Bernardo Strozzi (1581–1644), c. 1633 (Vienna, Musik-verein)

Cremona, a hint of local industry appearing in the violin and bow
suspended at the upper left. The visible ear and shape of the face
are his, also the large expressive eyes; perhaps only the nose does
not agree exactly with that in the later portraits. But by far the most
convincing genuflection to genuineness is made by the instrument
he holds, mentioned by his brother Giulio Cesare in the "Dichiara-
zione" printed in the *Scherzi musicali* of 1607. Claudio is said to
be heavily committed to music of many kinds, and to the study and
practice of two viole bastarde—probably referring to a pair with
two different tunings.

The viola bastarda was the queen of instruments for playing ornaments, as Francesco Rognoni tells us in the second part of his
highly diverting *Selva de varii passaggi* of 1620, published as an
expression of gratitude for time spent under the protection of Sigismund III, King of Poland. Its compass encouraged movement from
bass to alto range and the exploitation of imitative passages, yet the
basic sound was mellow, thriving on the long, sweet bow-strokes
that seem to be so essential an ingredient of Monteverdi's counterpoint.

Until further proof can be found, the Ashmolean portrait will
continue to tease us after the fashion of the finale of *Poppea*. Is it
really the master, or somebody very much like him? Of popular im-
ages, there is however one which for all its similarity to the composer must now be considered as false. It is the picture of an actor
with a mask and a look of *terribilità*, often reproduced from 1967
onwards when it was chosen as the frontispiece to their book *Claudio Monteverdi* by Guglielmo Barblan, Claudio Gallico and Guido
Pannain (Turin: ERI).

The reason for its popularity is clearly not its authenticity, for it
was shown to be a portrait of Tristano Martinelli, most famous of
Arlecchinos, in the early part of 1978. It is nevertheless a magnificent painting, the work of Domenico Fetti, well known both in
Mantua and in Venice. Although the story of this deception was told
by Pamela Askew in her article "Fetti's 'Portrait of an Actor' Reconsidered" (*The Burlington Magazine* 120, [1978]: 59–65), it is
still being foisted off as Monteverdi twenty years later and will
probably so continue. Its most recent reappearance is on the cover
of the *Rivista Illustrata del Museo Teatrale alla Scala* 23 (Summer
1994), an issue which oddly enough contains some excellent articles about the composer.

If a mistaken glance in 1967 has taken so long to deflect, it is also true, alas, that a genuine portrait first reproduced about then has so far remained virtually unrecognized. Why has identification taken so long? Perhaps because it appeared as the last of eighteen plates in a slim volume published to coincide with the celebration of the composer's tercentenary in Cremona in 1967: *Iconografia Monteverdiana,* by Elia Santoro, who has also written a book on the composer's early years. Both form part of the *Annali della Biblioteca Governativa e Libreria Civica di Cremona,* the biographical work as volume 18, 1967, and the iconographical study as volume 19, 1968.

I have found no mention of the portrait (reproduced of course only in black-and-white) in any Monteverdi literature known to me. The original, said to be in Bergamo, cannot now be traced. It is described as an anonymous painting of Claudio Monteverdi with musicians, the artist being possibly Mantuan, since the view from the window at the left shows what appears to be the city of the Gonzaga. The artist may however have been imported, as were at least two of the people present. The composer is seated at the right of a table laden with various instruments—a violin and bow, a slide

A portrait that may be of Monteverdi in his youth, and a portrait that is *not* of Monteverdi

trumpet, several wind instruments—and two open part-books. Amidst them all, apparently unperturbed, stands a puppy, whose chin and haunches are being chucked and patted by a lady and a gentleman. Not, I think, a rehearsal, but a conversation piece of the kind sometimes favored by artists interested in musical subjects.

Monteverdi's viola bastarda, resting on the floor, has its scroll near his left shoulder, while his left hand (with first finger extended) touches the fingerboard. He is well past his youth, as the graying beard and hair attest. His formal attire, a black robe, is perhaps the livery of mixed silk and floss-silk mentioned in his letter of December 2, 1608, and the tasseled collar is part of a court musician's dress.

Next to him sits the lady singer he had first heard in Mantua shortly after her arrival there on June 23, 1610. Adriana Basile, born in Posillipo about the year 1580, rapidly made a name for herself in Naples, Rome and Florence as a contralto with gifts so uncommon that listeners were electrified even when she quietly tuned her archlute. Monteverdi had heard the two most acclaimed divas of his day, Ippolita Marotta in Rome, and Francesca Caccini in Florence, but to his trained and sensitive ear, "la bell'Adriana" surpassed them both. She was to make such an impression on Duke Vincenzo, who had invited her to Mantua, that he created her a baroness and gave her an estate at Piancerreto near Monferrato.

The youth next to the diva, wearing the same kind of collar as Monteverdi, is probably his elder son Francesco, ten years old at the time. The younger son was only seven, and would later qualify as a doctor. But Francesco had already given proof of his musical aptitude, for a letter written by Monteverdi to Cardinal Gonzaga in Rome shortly before the portrait was done (January 22, 1611) says that he manages both trillo and ornaments quite well.

At the far left is Mutio Barone, Adriana's husband, who had accompanied her from Naples to Bracciano and Florence and all the way to Mantua. He was in constant contact with the Gonzaga in their widespread ramifications, and also entered into correspondence with the court secretaries Striggio and Marigliani. He too would share in the honors bestowed on his wife. Their daughter Leonora, named after the recently deceased Eleonora Gonzaga, was born in December 1611, and eventually surpassed her mother in beauty of character and voice. Concerts given in Rome in 1649 by Adriana and her daughters Leonora and Margherita made a remarkable impression on André Maugars, who claimed that he quite forgot his mortal condition and thought himself among the delights of the blessed.

And what of the dog? Its coat is white, with a mark here and there like an ermine *(armellin)*. Being persistent rather than dogmatic, as his correspondence shows, Monteverdi may have called it to mind once more when writing the trio "Taci, Armelin" for his noble friend from Treviso, Giovanni Battista Anselmi, whose anthology of 1624 presented it somewhat in the manner of the "frottoia o canzonetta allegra" once requested by Adriana of the Cardinal:

> Tace, Armelin, deh taci! Non mi sturbar
> Hor ch' innanzi al mio bene
> Son per dirle il mio duol e le mie pene.
>
> Tace, Armelin, deh taci! no mi latrar
> Che vo' provar furarle anco due baci.
> Ah, tu non vuoi tacer, animaletto
> Cerbero traditor dispettosetto.

[Shut up, Ermie! Don't disturb me now that in my beloved's presence I am about to tell her my sorrow and suffering. Shut up, Ermie! And don't bark, for I want to try snatching two more kisses. So you don't want to keep quiet, little animal? You mischievous traitor of a Cerberus!]

The portrait reproduced on the book jacket shows the composer as he may have looked during the last few years of his life, wearing the ordinary garb of a priest. It is the first time this painting has appeared in a publication.

Bernardo Strozzi's portrait (see page 133), made after the composer became a priest in 1632, soon became well-known, as is proved by Marco Boschini's reference in *La carta del Navegar Pitoresco*. The existence of one painting could certainly have attracted another artist intent on honouring a Venetian musical hero. The later portrait suggests a date between 1637 and 1642, for at that time Monteverdi began his last intensely active phase. Having corresponded with Giovanni Battista Doni, he completed the Eighth Book of Madrigals (dedicated to the Emperor Ferdinand III) and opened his most mature operatic period, which included *Ulisse, Poppea,* and a revival of *Arianna.* These events could account for Monteverdi's new and dapper look, for the somewhat bushy beard of c. 1632 has given way to a well-trimmed shorter version whose

A portrait of Monteverdi and friends in Mantua, spring 1611

shape would surely have met with the approval of his barber-surgeon father.

Always at ease in Venice, Monteverdi had said goodbye to the plague and the years of struggle. He had entered a final period of recognition and honor when his secular vocal music for Vienna, his *Selva morale* of 1640, and his operas transformed him into a new man. All this seems to be reflected in his physiognomy and appearance.

Knowing nothing of the provenance of the painting or the name of the artist, it is impossible for me to guess at the original circumstances. Such paintings were commonly made for wall-decoration of Italian conservatories; I seem to remember Monteverdi portraits of Bologna, Milan and Venice in the conservatories. Though independent of these, it does seem related to the color wash by Jan van Grevenbroch in the volumes headed *Abiti e Costumi Veneziani* in Venice's Museo Correr.

6

Monteverdi's Necklace

MANY YEARS AGO, *Nino Pirrotta planned a series of recitals of Monteverdi madrigals for the Terzo Programma of Radiotelevisione Italiana. Resulting from this radio series, rather than from any special research, two articles of his appeared in 1968 as* Scelte poetiche di Monteverdi *and were later augmented and translated as "Monteverdi's Poetic Choices" in the same author's* Music and Culture in Italy from the Middle Ages to the Baroque *(Cambridge, MA and London: 1984).*

On the cover of an offprint from the original Italian publication, he wrote a dedication followed by an evocatively satirical quatrain based on the opening sonnet of Book 7 by Giambattista Marino:

> Tempro la cetra, e per cantar gli onori
> di Monteverdi alzo lo stile e i carmi;
> ma invan la tento, et impossibil parmi
> ch'ella giammai risoni altro che . . . orrori. . . .

Continuing to sing Monteverdi's honors, Pirrotta has made a splendid contribution to our better comprehension of the poetry underlying the musical settings. His preliminary study of 1968 inspired me to investigate the background of the Seventh Book and its links with other works produced about the same time.

My study, published in *The Musical Quarterly* in 1973, appears in a new guise. The opening material, with its guesswork about two madrigals mentioned in a letter of 1607, is now revised and enriched by Anthony Pryer's article "Monteverdi, two sonnets and a letter" (*Early Music* 25 [1997]), where harmonic and contrapuntal devices are analyzed in relation to the premiere of the contemporaneous *Orfeo,* with new evidence about the influence of a passage from Cavalieri's *Rappresentatione di Anima et di Corpo* of 1600.

141

D I N C E R T O

Sul MONTE, Che dà Terra al Cielo afcefo
    Dal Regno di Giunon la cima altera
    Eftolle sì, ch'eterna Primauera
    Gode, ne ma ida fero turbo .è offefo

C L A V D I O Lieue n'afcendi, ed iui apprefo
    Il Canto e'l fuon dà quefta è quella sfera,
    Doppia Armonia fi dolce, e Lufinghera,
    Rechi, ch'in Terra il Ciel fembra difcefo:

Ma che? ful giogo altrui poggiar non dei
    MONTE VERDE Ch'al Ciel frondeggi apprefso,
    Tu il viuo Olimpo à te medefmo fei.

Ben tua Lingua , e tua man fcoprono efprefso
    Mentre molci gli Orecchi è l'Alme bei,
    Che foura te fouente alzi te ftefso .

Onto the mountain which rises from earth to heaven
    and so extols the lofty heights of Juno's kingdom
    that it enjoys eternal spring,
    and never is disturbed by savage throng,

Claudio cheerfully climbs, and learning there
    the song and sound of this sphere and that,
    brings a double harmony so sweet and persuasive
    that heaven seems to come down to earth.

What's this? on no other peak can you place
    Monteverdi, who shoots forth leaves so near to heaven,
    you are a living Olympus yourself.

Your tongue, your hand reveal themselves expressed
    while suavely you soothe both ear and soul,
    which often you raise above yourself.

      Anonymous poem prefaced to the *Seventh Book of Madrigals.*

Facsimile of a poem prefaced to *Madrigals, Book 7,* with translation

This is the miracle of Monteverdi research. Look for evidence of his activity in madrigals, and you find that simultaneously he is seeing through the press a book of songs by a young composer from Cremona, or music for St. John Baptist, or writing an opera on a libretto of more than 1,000 lines by the Mantuan court secretary Ercole Marigliani. This work, entitled *Andromeda,* was partly rediscovered in the mid-1980s when Albi Rosenthal acquired a unique copy of the libretto and described it in his article "Monteverdi's 'Andromeda': a Lost Libretto found" (*Music & Letters* 66 [1985]). Let us hope that eventually the music will reappear.

*   *   *

Monteverdi's extant correspondence, rich in references to the operas, ballets, and other stage works written for Mantua, Parma, and Venice, provides in contrast precious little information about his church music and even less about his madrigals. In some ways this is surprising, and even disappointing, since his work for chapel and chamber spreads itself as generously and evenly over his long career as does the stage music; but in other ways it is only to be expected, because a motet or a madrigal—being considerably less complex than a work *in genere rappresentativo,* with all its problems of production—needs less discussion and therefore does not call for a special or detailed letter to the recipient of the music.

In fact, the only book of madrigals referred to in the correspondence with any degree of certainty is the seventh, and even this is never mentioned by number, or by name (*Concerto*), but rather by a variety of self-effacing diminutives such as "mia operetta,"[1] "certe mie musichette," or "miei deboli canti." In rare moments of courage they become "li miei libri," or "li miei madrigali." Of course, isolated and self-contained works are sometimes mentioned long before publication occurs, as in the case of the ballet *Tirsi e Clori;* and this finds a parallel in a brief reference to the *Combattimento di Tancredi e Clorinda* in a letter (no. 92) dated May 1, 1627, although the work did not appear in print until 1638. There is also the fascinating case of the madrigals discussed, but not named, in a

---

1. *The Letters of Claudio Monteverdi,* translated and introduced by Denis Stevens (Oxford: Clarendon Press, 1995), nos. 34ff. Further citations by letter number.

much earlier letter (no. 4) sent to the court councillor Annibale Iberti on July 28, 1607.[2]

This correspondence bypassed Mantua completely, since Monteverdi was resting in Cremona while Iberti, with Duke Vincenzo and the court, was spending the summer at Sampierdarena, then a well-wooded spa near Genoa. With the duke at this time was a group of his court singers, directed by a certain Don Bassano—presumably the Don Bassano Casola whose musical powers had been rewarded by a lucrative appointment as official weigher of bread in the city of Mantua.[3] The beginning of the letter makes it clear that Monteverdi had waited for the duke to leave before departing for a much-needed holiday in Cremona, and it is also clear that he had not expected any summer commissions, for even a madrigal took six days to write, and another two days for trying it out and recopying it.

The multiple references to Book 7 mostly occur in 1619 (the year of first publication) and 1620, and they usually mention the dedicatee—Caterina Medici Gonzaga—by her title of Duchess of Mantua. There were several reasons why Monteverdi should wish to dedicate this compilation, the fruit of five years' work, to the duchess. She was the wife of his patron and admirer Duke Ferdinand, who had never ceased to regret the hasty action of his brother Francesco in dismissing Monteverdi in July 1612. Moreover she was a Medici, like her illustrious predecessor Eleonora (the second wife of Monteverdi's first Mantuan patron, Duke Vincenzo), and the memory of "Madama Leonora che sià in gloria" is evoked in a letter to Striggio when the idea of a formal presentation is first mooted. She was undoubtedly acquainted with Monteverdi's music long before her marriage, which took place in Florence on February 7, 1617, and she may even have been partly responsible for suggesting that Monteverdi should compose something for the occasion.

Most important of all, perhaps, is the sad fact that Monteverdi did not attend the wedding, although his old friend Rinuccini had invited him to stay at his house, nor did he write any music for the

2. For a detailed reassessment of these works, see Anthony Pryer, "Monteverdi, two sonnets and a letter," *Early Music* 25 (1997): 357–71.

3. Antonio Bertolotti, *Musici alla corte dei Gonzaga in Mantova* (Milan: 1890), 72. This volume should be used only in the light of a review by Emil Vogel in *Vierteljahrsschrift für Musikwissenschaft* 7 (1921): 279–84. Don Bassano Casola, a native of Lodi, made a great success of his career in Mantua and was a close friend of the singer Francesco Rasi, whose *Vaghezze di musica per una voce sola* (Venice: 1608) he collected and introduced.

wedding. *Nozze di Tetide* had been begun and then as soon abandoned; and if other works were commissioned by way of substitute, Monteverdi did not travel to Mantua in order to rehearse and direct them in the presence of the newlyweds, because the jealousy of certain local musicians (in particular, Sante Orlandi) caused plans to be canceled. It is quite possible, however, that he sent music, at Striggio's request, for a concert celebrating the return of Ferdinando and Caterina to Mantua on March 7, for there are several works in Book 7 that would be appropriate for a time of rejoicing.

Caterina's lineage, her marriage to the duke, her love of music, would have been enough to prompt such a dedication as Monteverdi had in mind. But the disappointment over the wedding music must surely have been the deciding factor, transforming a pious thought into a far-reaching action, and gathering together solos, duets, trios, quartets, quintets, and sextets into a new kind of madrigal book—a melange of love songs, occasional pieces, court music, and ballet, in all of which the continuo is not an optional element, but a necessary one.

Apart from the well-known letter about *Tirsi e Clori* (no. 16), the first hint of the anthology appears in a letter to Striggio (October 19, 1619), Monteverdi complaining that the printer has failed to meet the agreed deadline for publication:

> If the printer, as indeed he promised, had handed over to me my little publication, I would already have presented it to Her Highness (to whom it is dedicated) so as to be able to obtain through her infinite kindness and humanity that favor which was also granted to me by the Most Serene Lady Eleonora—may she be in glory!—that is, her kindness in counting me among the number of her humblest, indeed, but also devoted and faithful servants: a favor which guaranteed me certain help (and genuine too, through being really deserved for once) from that small endowment or property from which I have been able to draw the income that I greatly need—little though it is—of 100 scudi given to me by His Highness Duke Vincenzo of glorious memory.
>
> But the tardiness of that printer has been and is even now the reason why I am not in Mantua, and have not gone. I hope however it will be ready by the 8th or 10th of next month. If His Highness Duke Ferdinando has not left for Casale, as in a short time he will—so it is rumored here—I shall then come to present it, and at the same time I shall bring you at least the greater part (if not all) of Your Lordship's eclogue, set to music by me. (No. 34)

The printer turned out to be even more dilatory than Monteverdi had surmised, for the part-books were not off the press until December 13, and by that time traveling conditions were more difficult and there was the usual Christmas Eve Mass to be written and rehearsed. On that date in December, Monteverdi sat at his writing desk, with his advance copies of *Concerto* before him, and wrote to Striggio:

> I have in readiness a little publication of mine to present to Her Most Serene Ladyship, and I am waiting for her return for this carnival; for if she were not to return, I would decide to send it rather than bring it, as indeed I shall do if she comes to Mantua. (No. 35)

The pattern is all too familiar. Monteverdi is ready and willing to set out for Mantua, but something unforeseen prevents him from doing so. He feels unwell, the weather has taken a turn for the worse, there is much to do at S. Marco, he is not sure whether to come because the duke and duchess may have left for the country. But he cannot be blamed entirely, for it was between Mantua and Venice (at a lonely and rather ominous spot about two miles from Sanguinetto) that he was robbed, together with his son and a maid-servant, in the autumn of 1613; and having irretrievably lost both goods and money, all of them hard-earned over a long and exhausting period of his life, he had obviously decided that while he would never admit to a dislike of travel, he would always devise a means of avoiding it if humanly possible. Striggio knew this perhaps better than anyone, and he was certainly astute enough to read between Monteverdi's hastily written lines. A few more were sent on January 16, 1620:

> I understand that Her Highness will soon be in Mantua, and I too hope to be in Mantua to present certain of my little musical pieces to her. In whatever way you deem it good, I shall be bound to serve you with all my heart. (No. 39)

As Monteverdi grew older, he became (like Beethoven) an adept at serving more than one master. Admittedly a touch of pluralism was necessary for survival, and Monteverdi therefore managed to keep the procurators of S. Marco reasonably happy, while at the same time dealing with various printers and publishers, writing music on commission for Venetian churches and confraternities, going to Parma to provide music for stage and spectacle, keeping up a brisk correspondence with Mantua, and entering into a new and fruitful relationship with Paolo Giordano II, Duke of Bracciano, in Rome. This concerned one of the Duke's musicians, the lutenist-composter Francesco Petratti, whose book of songs Monteverdi (a fellow-Cremonese) had been asked to see through the press. One of the letters to the Duke mentions Book 7, a copy having already been dispatched to Bracciano.

> I also write to beseech you kindly to accept the copy of my little madrigals (now published) that I sent directly to the Signor Cavaliere by the previous post, so that he could present it to Your Excellency in my name, begging you to have regard more to my devotion than to their little merit. (No. 40)

The letter to Rome bears the date January 25, 1620, and a week later Monteverdi wrote to Striggio about the music for *Apollo,* once more talking of a visit to Mantua which had to be abandoned because of Marigliani's *Andromeda:*

> I was thinking of travelling to Mantua to present my books—which I have now had printed—dedicated to Her Highness (to take an advantageous road that may lead me to the goal I so much desired and worked for), so as to be able, once and for all, to get possession of that small donation which His Highness Duke Vincenzo, of beloved memory, was kind enough to grant me.
> But remembering that Signor Marigliani's play[4] would have fallen entirely on my shoulders—and knowing that with the passage of time a feeble branch can bear a huge fruit, so that in no time at all the ability to hold up without breaking would be out of the question—in order not to break myself (in my feeble state of health), I did not want to come at such short notice to sustain this impossible weight, because something other than haste is needed to do justice to such a project, and it is no small matter to make a success of it even with plenty of time. (No. 42)

By the next post, a week later, Monteverdi's intentions become perfectly clear: he wants Striggio to present the part-books to the duchess, and make such apologies and excuses as may be necessary. This letter is dated February 8, 1620.

---

4. Ercole Marigliani's contribution entitled *Andromeda* was set to music under great pressure. Although the music is lost, a libretto was discovered and discussed by Albi Rosenthal, "Monteverdi's 'Andromeda': a Lost Libretto Found," *Music & Letters* 66 (1985): 1–8.

If you, however, are unable at present to honor me with further commands, I shall still not refrain from begging you a favor, which is that you may be so kind as to present, in my name, to Her Most Serene Ladyship, those madrigals dedicated to her, which I thought of presenting in person had I been able to come to Mantua; but the obvious impediments prevent me from doing so.

I shall arrange for these books (if you will so kindly do me the honor of assisting me) to be handed over personally to Your Lordship by my father-in-law. More than this I was not hoping to do even if I came myself, other than to commend myself to Her Highness's favour and protection, so that one of these days I might be rewarded by His Highness the Duke so as to be able to have my capital, from which I could draw my annual pension. (No. 42)

The final explosion is still to come. On February 22, Monteverdi returns to the attack, pointing out that, whereas Duke Vincenzo rewarded him with a donation (no strings being attached), the Mantuan administrators always talk about future payments but avoid giving him what is due now. But he goes on to express his gratitude to Striggio for promising to present the madrigals.

You would therefore do me a favor, Your Lordship, by forgiving me if I do not come at once (because of the said obstacles) to obey your commands; and since you have kindly honored me with a promise to present my madrigals—in my name—to her Ladyship, they have just been sent off to my father-in-law. He will come and bring these to Your Lordship and will be at your service as far as Her Ladyship's residence. But I beg you to offer an apology for me, the reasons for which are the obstacles I have just mentioned, and assure her that I am her most humble and devoted servant, and that I commend myself in this business of mine to Her Highness's infinite kindness. (No. 45)

Monteverdi was playing "hard to get," but whether he really wanted at any point in his Venetian career to return to the Gonzagas for good is doubtful to say the least. What he did want was the transfer of his *fondo,* or capital, so that he could invest it well with the merchant bankers of Venice and so draw his annual pension regularly and without effort or embarrassment. While it remained in Mantua, guarded by jealous treasury officials, his chances of enjoying its modest income were small. One of the duke's musicians, Francesco Dognazzi, had approached Monteverdi in November 1619 with the offer of a return to service in Mantua; but the words were whispered abroad in the narrow alleys and broad piazzas of

Venice, until one day early in February 1620, when Monteverdi hinted that he might be going to Mantua for the purpose of handing a presentation copy of *Concerto* to the duchess, no less a dignitary than the Dean of S. Marco posed a somewhat sharply pointed question.

The Most Illustrious Primicerius, son of the Most Excellent Lord Procurator, My Lord of the House of Cornaro, said to me: "This business of your going to Mantua—they say you are going there for good!"

And this, perhaps, was one of the main reasons that kept me from bringing those books in person, because (dear Sir) the substance is bound to be dearer to me than the accident. (No. 48)

Now we realize why Monteverdi wrote, in his letter of February 8, requesting Striggio to take over the entire little ceremony of presentation. It was not a case of pressure of work, but rather pressure of opinion, that prevented the composer from performing this agreeable task himself. He had chosen as dedicatee of his first truly Venetian anthology not a patron or patriarch of that fair city, which had offered him shelter, office, and honors, but a patroness living in another city and ruling over another state; and to make matters worse he had every intention of leaving his duties for a week and traveling to Mantua to hand over the prize. If this were really the way in which tongues were wagging, no wonder Monteverdi decided to stay at home. But Striggio, touched by the plea to perform the honors in the presence of the duchess, and struck by the quality and beauty of the music (which he certainly had time to try over privately between the receipt of the part-books and the time when he handed them over), obtained from the duke an authorization to approach Monteverdi once again on the subject of coming back to Mantua as *maestro di cappella e di musica da camera*. The reply, dated March 8, thanks Striggio profusely but pleads for time in which to consider the offer.

Then comes the longest letter Monteverdi ever penned, at least among his extant correspondence. In more than six closely-written pages he carefully goes over every point of the offer: how much he earns at S. Marco, and how much more this is than the salary of his eminent predecessors; how much he earns by accepting commissions from outside, and how he is thanked warmly as well as paid promptly. In addition to financial security and artistic opportunity, he enjoys a position of power in the elaborate hierarchy of the doge's private chapel: it is up to him to appoint or dismiss musicians (in actual fact he would ask for the advice of the three *procuratori de supra*),[5] and he need not attend every service requiring music if he does not wish to, since he has a capable assistant to stand in for him.

Against all this he weighs the Mantuan offer, which involves a certain amount of currency conversion, and decides that it is not really worth very much. It seems that the duke would only go as far as matching Monteverdi's annual income from S. Marco, and even this involved some kind of trickery, for only two-thirds of the sum was guaranteed, the other third coming from ground rents assigned to him by the treasury. Indignantly, Monteverdi points out that this part of the income is his already, allocated to him by Duke Vincenzo; and how can he be given what is already his by right? He also contrasts the security of his Venetian post with the fact that Mantua's proferred patronage could cease with the death or displeasure of the duke. After all, it was the death of Vincenzo that caused trouble in the first place, and the displeasure of his successor Francesco that finally severed the fraying bond of loyalty in 1612.

Still overcome by a sense of injustice, Monteverdi cites the generous rewards given to eminent singers—Adriana Basile, Francesco Campagnolo, Bassano Casola—and compares their affluence to his own penury while in Mantua. His observations may be lacking in tact (if it is tactless to discuss the salaries paid to others), but they are not far short of the truth. Adriana Basile, her husband and her sisters were so well paid by the Gonzagas for a few years' work that they were able to retire comfortably on the proceeds, while Monteverdi, much older than they, had twenty more years of toil ahead. Matters of honor, of family, of finance and (not least important) contractual matters finally spell out the verdict: he will come to Mantua on his own terms, not on those of the duke. And the letter ends with yet another reference to *Concerto:*

> Forgive me, Your Lordship, if I have gone on for too long. There remains nothing for me to do at present other than to thank Your Lordship from the bottom of my heart for the singular favor done to me in having presented my madrigals to Her Higness, and I am sure that through the

5. These were responsible for the administration of the income of the basilica. They also chose assistants to the clergy, engaged musicians and guarded the treasury and archives.

most honourable medium of Your Lordship they will have been much more acceptable and welcome.

In April 1620, we find two letters referring to *Concerto*—one to Striggio and the other to the duchess. Both were written on the same day, April 14, and it is clear from the context that the letter to the duchess was enclosed with the one to Striggio, who is requested to look it over and (if all is in order) to have it sealed and delivered (no. 53). In this way Monteverdi could be sure that the duchess was properly thanked for the necklace[6] she had sent him by way of recognition of his dedicating the madrigals to her.

> I do not know whether I have done well or not in having written the enclosed letter to Her Ladyship by way of thanks for being so kind as to grant me such an outstanding favor (through the medium of Your Lordship's special protection), she having sent me by courier that beautiful necklace as a gift. Your Lordship will do me a favor by giving it a glance, and if you consider it suitable I entreat Your Lordship to have it sealed and to present it to her. (No. 54)

Although it has sometimes been hinted that Monteverdi's letters lack punctuation, and are occasionally deficient in such matters as good grammar and syntax, a study of the originals reveals hitherto unsuspected details. In the best of his letters, internal structure and balance of phrase come very near to the quality of his musical structure, which not infrequently combines power and subtlety to a remarkable degree. This episode closes with a brief mention, in the letter to Striggio dated May 10, 1620 (no. 56), of a friendly reply from the duchess:

> I received a most gracious reply to my letter, through Her Ladyship's infinite kindness, and this singular favor alone was (without any other

---

6. The gift of a necklace to a musician was by no means unusual, as is shown by other letters of this period. Caccini was presented with one by the Duke of Ferrara in 1592, as is proved by a letter from Emilio de' Cavalieri to Luzzasco Luzzachi. See Henry Prunières, "Une lettre inédite d'Emilio, del Cavaliere," in *La Revue musicale* 4 (1923): 131–33. This is not to deny the fact that Monteverdi occasionally sent a small gift to the duchess. He did so in April 1622, when he presented her with a rare and remarkable monkey that had been brought from Egypt by a relative. But this was by way of thanks for a favour she had done him by arranging for his son Massimiliano to enter Cardinal Mont'Alto's college in Bologna.

recognition) sufficient to make me perforce her lifelong servant. But I am not so modest a connoisseur of the truth as not to realize that the greater part of my credit as regards Her Highness's favor springs from Your Lordship's special protection.

The relationship between Monteverdi and Striggio remained good until the end, because it was more than a means of communication between a mere musician and a count (later a marquis) who held such high offices as Grand Chancellor and Lord President of the Magistracy. The friendship, loyalty, and artistic communion born of their work together on *L'Orfeo* in 1607 served for twenty years as an anchor in a frequently stormy sea, and if Monteverdi behaved at times (when under severe provocation) like an enraged Neptune, it was Striggio who calmed the waves and set matters to right.

What became of the necklace? Monteverdi had no close female relatives to whom he could pass it on, and he was not so hard pressed for money that he was obliged at any time to sell it for cash. Although he may have received other necklaces as gifts, there is no mention in his correspondence apart from the duchess's gift made in 1620, and it is therefore highly probable that the "collana di cento ducati" mentioned in a letter to Strigio (January 1, 1628) may be the one he had carefully put aside for eight years in case of sudden need.

The need in 1628 was not only sudden but dire, as far as Monteverdi was concerned. His son Massimiliano, having become a doctor of medicine with a small practice in Mantua, was denounced by a colleague to the Father Inquisitor, the charge being one of reading a forbidden book. Although Massimiliano pleaded that he did not know the book was forbidden, he was told that his temporary release could only be obtained by the deposition of a pledge of one hundred ducats. Monteverdi lost no time in searching out the necklace and taking it to a Venetian jeweler he knew and could trust:

> The favor which I now beg of Your Lordship's great authority, with all due affection, is this: only that you may be so kind as to influence the Father Inquisitor so that he lets Massimiliano go back home, by virtue of the pledge which he himself requested of me. I desire nothing else of Your Lordship's grace, since I have handed over a necklace worth 100 ducats to Signor Barbieri (a rich dealer in precious stones who is here in Venice, both a countryman of mine, and a close friend for many years), so that he may write by this post asking Signor Zavare-

lla, who looks after the customs duties of His Most Serene Highness of Mantua and is a very close friend of the aforesaid Signor Barbieri, to come to Your Lordship and offer to look after the pledge personally. (No. 116)

A postscript to the letter tells Striggio that the Mantuan intermediary will be the duke's jeweler, Signor Spiga, instead of Signor Zavarella. But Striggio had forestalled Monteverdi's action by sending a pledge himself—a kind deed that drew from Monteverdi (January 9) an almost passionate letter of gratitude and devotion (no. 117). At the end of his letter of February 4, he returns to the subject again, hoping that the money will have been paid over and Striggio thus relieved of his financial responsibility:

> I entrusted Signor Barbieri, a rich merchant of Venice, to do his best to relieve Your Lordship of the pledge made for Massimiliano, and to this end he is keeping on hand for you a necklace worth 100 ducats. I am waiting for a reply about this: may Your Lordship forgive me for the delay. (No. 118)

The last two letters to Striggio deal with continuing troubles, for although the Father Inquisitor received the pledge, he was not willing at first to release Massimiliano unconditionally. "For how long do you wish your son to be released?" he asked Monteverdi, and the sorely tried, sixty-year-old composer, who had wept daily for the plight of his son, told Striggio: "How long? For ever"— begging him to help straighten out this twisted affair now that the Holy Office was apparently assured of Massimiliano's innocence. Eventually the composer's prayers and the chancellor's contrivings bore fruit, and Massimiliano returned to his practice, saved from the hangman's noose by the duchess's necklace—or nearly so. The curtain falls on his career in 1661, when the records of the parish of SS. Siro e Sepolcro contain the following entry:

> Don Massimiliano Monteverdi, physician aged about 57, after receiving the Holy Sacraments, Confession, Communion and holy oil, passed to a better life [and was] buried in Santo Nazaro on October 14.[7]

---

7. Giuseppe Pontiroli, *Notizie sui Monteverdi* (Cremona: 1968), 55.

7

Fiori Poetici—A Facsimile

SCHOLARS *searching for Monteverdian topics in the new millennium would do well to investigate clues hidden in the 70-page book entitled* Fiori Poetici, *preserved in the Biblioteca Nazionale di San Marco in Venice, where it is listed under "Miscellanea 1399, no. 23."*

My belief in its importance is proved by the following facsimile, in which most of the show-through due to heavy inking on thin paper has been minimalised. The only re-touching occurs on p. 28, where a crinkle had obscured a name rhyming with "vaso," which I supplied as "Pegaso" from the story of the Hippocrene.

Some parts of the opening *Laconismo* ("summing-up," or funeral eulogy) appear in Paolo Fabbri's standard biography (Turin: 1985) and in the translation by Dr. Tim Carter (Cambridge: 1994). Otherwise nothing much seems to have been done. Caberloti, priest though he was, stressed the role of Fate in Monteverdi's life by stating that "Fate gave him this name [Claudio], since he enclosed within himself so much that was significant." The composer himself would certainly have agreed, as he makes painfully clear in his letter to Annibale Chieppio on December 2, 1608.

* * *

By the spring of 2000, no modern edition or facsimile of the *Fiori Poetici* had appeared despite considerable interest shown by students of Monteverdi. After his death on November 29, 1643, Giovanni Rovetta directed an elaborate and moving Requiem in S. Marco, and a few days later came a second tribute organized by Monteverdi's Paduan friend Giovanni Battista Marinoni in the Church of the Frari. The funeral eulogy by Mateo Caberloti, parish priest of S. Tomà, prompted writers within and beyond the city to compose in memory of the great musician poems, acrostics, musico-literary devices and arithmetical puzzles in Italian and Latin. These were assembled into a book, with a title page by Giacomo Decini, which came out under the imprint of Francesco Miloco in 1644.

More than a score of Monteverdi's friends had sent in their homage and tribute. They ranged from famous figures such as Antonio di Vescovi, the well-known historian Francesco Bolano and the Rodiseo brothers, to foreigners from Bergamo, Padua and Urbino.

There are no eminent musicians among their number; but when in 1971 Igor Stravinsky's funeral rites were observed in Venice, composers were conspicuous by their absence; nor can I think of any post-cadential harmonic wreath offered him by younger contemporaries who can scarcely have flourished without his powerful influence.

I believe that some of these now faded poetical flowers hold a hitherto unperceived message about Monteverdi. Perhaps one day that message will be revealed.

INDEX OF AUTHORS

28	Pindo, non è più Pindo, il Lauro è secco	P.
29	O voi, che d'Ippocrene al sacro fonte	D. Ambrosio Rossi
30	Se giace in questa Tomba Apollo il sacro	[Rossi]
31	Giace trà petre il Monte	Padre Bac. Simon Olmo
31	Verdeggiante Corone	Simon Olmo
32	Da questi chiostri parte	anon
33	Note confuse, Parti sconcertate	P[aulo] P[iazza]
34	Claudio? chiuso sei quì? Morto nò. Vivi	anon
35	Posero già, per moveral Ciel guerra	Fra Ottavio Ragucci
36	Non si dolgan viventi	D. Alfonso Griloti
37	L'empireo è un monte, & la Gloria un verde	Padre Maestro Antonio Adami
38	Dal Cielo fregolato era il concento	Padre Maestro Antonio Adami
39	Per terminar, a chi si deve il pregio	G.A.N.A.
40	La Musica veggeva Claudio in Terra	Antonio de Vescovi
41	Dolor, che preme il petto, a l'Alma asserra	D. Alfonso Griloti
42	Com'hai tu Parca ria lo stame inciso	anon
43	In questa Tomba giace il MonteVerde	anon
44	Già s'è oscurato il Sole	anon
45	Tinse musico incanto	Guerino Rodiseo
47	Tu, che si grati honori	Di Alfonso Griloto
48	Sospirò Apollo, e di dolor ripieno	Pietro Maurici
49	Aeternum hic tacet, aeternum hic iacet	Iacobus Pighettus
50	Tempus ad antiquis tumulis sua iura reposcit	anon
51	Claudius Mons Viridis obiit	Franciscus Bolanus
52	Audierat musicos Orpheum	Reverendus Ludovicus Battalea
53	Lacte Cremona aluit, compressit Mantua morbo	Reverendus Ludovicus Battalea
54	Pharmaca desinit unquam mortalibus aegris	Reverendus Ludovicus Battalea
55	Claudius en obiit, iacet en quoq[ue] Claudius ille	Reverendus Ludovicus Battalea
56	Olim Mons viridis resonans Virtute canorus	anon
57	Vos Aonidum chori, proceres modulaminum	Franciscus Rodiseus
58	Monte isto in Viridi cecinit modo Cycnus Aedon	Balthasar Bonifacius
59	Excita frondolis Aoniae lucis funestas Melpomene	anon
60	Hei mihi, quid celebris tam Virtus Adepta labore	anon
61	Anagramma: Laudent corde Iovem	Antonius de Episcopis
62	Anagramma: Iove cantu mel reddo	Antonius de Episcopis
63	Vaticinium Arithmeticum	Antonius de Episcopis
64	Conversa est laetitia in luctum	D. Alphonsus Grillotus
65	Mons Viridis Terra liquit, Celumq[ue] petivit	Marc'Antonius Romitus

66	Vaticinium Arithmeticum: Claudio Monteverde	Antonius de Episcopis
67	Fuor dell'Alghe marine	D. Alfonso Grillotti
68	Cadè, perche la Parca, Troncando il fil vitale	D. Alfonso Grillotti
69	Stupisce huomeni, e belve	Bernardo Moscatelo
69	Trà le più scielte schiere	Bernardo Moscatelo
70	Sonetto musicale: [Lunga] è la pena	Paulo Piazza
[71]	Al Lettore	

LIST OF CONTRIBUTORS

Anon, 15, 24, 32, 34, 42–44, 50, 56, 59, 60
A., G.A.N., 39
Adami, Antonio, Padre Maestro, Logico Publico di Padova, 37, 38
Battalea, Rev. Lodovico, 52–55
Bolano, Francisco, patr. Ven., 51
Bonifacio, Balthasare, 57
Caberloti, Matteo, piovan di S. Tomà, 5, 13
Grilotti, D. Alfonso, (Targa, nobile Urbinato), 19, 25, 27, 36, 41, 47, 64, 67, 68
Maurici, Pietro, Monc. Fer. Min. Con., 48
Mauritius, Fr, 17, 18
Moscatelo, Bernardo, 69
Olmo, Padre Bac. Simon, 31
P., 28
Piazza, Padre Maestro Paolo, 14, 21, 22, 26, 33, 70
Pighettus, Iacobus, patritius Bergomas, 49
Quadrario, Rev. Don Pietro, piovan in S. Giacomo d'Oro, 16
Raguzzi, Fra Ottavio, 35
Rodiseo, Francisco, 57
Rodiseo, Guerino, 45
Rossi, D. Ambrosio, 29, 30
Romito, Marc'Antonio, 65
Vescovi, Antonio di, 20, 40, 61, 62, 63, 66

ALLI ILLVSTRISSIMI,

ET ECCELLENTISSIMI SIGNORI

FRANCESCO MOLINI

PROCVRATOR:

GIOVANNI NANI

PROCVRATOR, E CAVALIER:

GIOVANNI PESARO

PROCVRATOR, E CAVALIER.

PEr eternarmi obligato al debito de' riceuuti beneficŋ̃ dal Molto Illuſtre, e Molto Reuerendo Signor Clau-dio Monteuerde non hò ritrouato mezzo il più pro-prio, che ridotte inſieme le di lui cantate lodi in vario metro da Poeti de' noſtri tempi conſecrarle al nome dell' Eccellenze Voſtre Illuſtriſſme, perche ſon ſicuro, che la loro auttorità rendendole conſpicue, e meriteuoli d' vn' vniuerſale accetto, e rimanendo aggradite, ne riceuerò in vn *medesimo tempo doppio il frutto della mia ben impiegata gratitudine: poiche hauendo nella Ducale di S. Marco per elettione di Vostre Eccellenze Illustrissime sotto la di lui regentia doppiamente seruito per cantore con questo tributo di affettuosa deuotione confido, c'hauerò corrisposo all'officio di vn ben disciplinato scholare, & in qualche parte nella confessione de gl'infiniti miei oblighi spero meritar perenne il possesso della gratia di Vostre Eccellenze, della quale benche lontano vino desiderosissimo. Intanto angurandole la dinturnità de gl'anni Nestorei humilissimo all'Eccellenze Vostre Illustrissime m'inchino.*

Di Padoua li 25. Maggio 1644.

DI VOSTRE ECCELLENZE ILLVSTRISSIME

Humilissimo, e deuotissimo Scrittore

Gio: Battista Marinoni.

LA-

LACONISMO
DELLE ALTE QVALITA'
DI CLAVDIO MONTEVERDE.

DEL MOLTO ILLVSTRE, E REVERENDISSIMO

MATTEO CABERLOTI

PIOVAN DI S. THOMA'.

****

N On hà confini l'eloquenza, e donando a' viuenti in riguardo de' gloriosi gesti l'immortalità, quasi fiume perenne, anzi mare immenso non manca d'abbondante copia delle sue dolcezze à chi l'assaggia, nè nega partito d'inoltrarsi à nuoue nauigatióni à chi le tenta. Le lodi scarsamente non si dispensano, quando all'ampiezza de' meriti s'offerisce Oratóre, il quale all'orecchio d'Ascoltanti con ordine ben inteso sà rappresentarle. E' poca Fortuna di quel mortale, che doppo diuturne fatiche per impossessarsi della Virtù, fatto glorioso, e degno d'vn nome non soggetto à morte, per mancanza di spiegante i meritati pregi, soccombi ad vn'ingrato silentio delle rari sue doti. Mà chi può promettersi (ò Signori) in breue giro di mal composta oratióne sufficientemente commendare quel soggetto, che porgerebbe abbondeuole materia à ben giusti volumi, e stancarebbe la facondia de' più sperimentati dicitori? E' stolto, chi crede di volar senz'ali, ed ogni Vccello non può già penetrar le nubi. Con-

tengasi

teneifi ogn'uno più tosto d'ammirare l'altezza dell'ingegno di Claudio, che di tentare con discapito di se medesimo vn scarso racconto dell'inenarrabili qualità, che come più, che humane renisarono costui tra gli huomeni vn semideo. Questi tra peritissimi Mufici de suoi giorni fù prima pratticato per dotto Maestro, che conosciuto scholare imparante i primi Musicali principij di modo, che nella sua fiorita giouentù capitando al seruitio de' Serenissimi di Mantoua diede, che pensare ad ascoltanti la diuinità delle sue compolixioni, che accommiatateli in vn medesimo tratto da Parnaso le due sorelle la Poesia, e Musica, nel Monte Verde, del Cremonese, quiui soggiornando procurassero in Claudio appunto racchiuder tutte le glorie della passata antichità, e come essemplare d'imitatione appoggiata ad vn non plus vltra lasciarlo alla posterità. Hebbe non và dubbio, e francamente si caua da Lucretio hauer hauuta origine la Mufica dall'osseruanza de gl'huomeni, come anche l'arte Oratoria; e però chi con occhio ben purgato dell'intelletto la mira, e contempla, deue confessarla dono del Cielo, parto diuino; arte più d'ogn'altra commendabile, insegnata dalla natura à gl'Vccelli, facendo con variati modi souemente sentire il perfetto artificio d'vn'armonioso canto. Di quest'arte fauorito da Apollo il nostro Claudio comparue alle Corti Serenissime di Mantoua, e Parma, e quiui de nobilissimi ingegni ritrouati componimenti Poetici, che muti ne loro numeri non compartiuano à gl'animi de Prencipi quelle affettioni, le quali desiauano; Claudio col numero armonioso, ò musicale misura conseguì quel più, che à niun mortale di Mufica professante puote esser già mai concesso. Ritrouossi alle già dette Corti Serenissime in tempo di Nozze, e mentre gl'animi di tutti s'apparecchiauano alle allegrezze: poco loro giouaua, se con varij modi di Mufica non compartiua loro il diletto questo altissimo ingegno; poiche come perfettissimo possessore del numero armonico col Dorio persuadeua la prudenza, e cagionaua ne petti desiderij di casti pensieri; col Frigio prouocaua alle pugna quei spiriti de Prencipi viuaci, e gl'infiammaua i cuori de furiosi voti. Con l'Eolio tranquillaua le tempeste, e procelle interne de gl'animi, e participaua alle volontà pacificate il sonno, e la quiete: col Lidio finalmente auniua a gl'intelletti, e sgrauandoli del desiderio di cose terrene, gli moueua l'appetito delle 'celesti, e così egregiamente adoperadosi partoriua mille beni. Puote, ò Signori,

ne

ae tempi di Pitagora quella cantatrice col canto de Spondei rallentare la prestezza de gl'animi, raddolcire la rabbie de cuori, e con la grauità della Melodia raffettare i conceputi sdegni. Prouauano i Lacedemoni nella misura Cromatica effeminarsi gl'animi della loro giouentù: Et Homero col modo musico appreso da Chirone dolcemente violentaua Achille à deporre il sdegno. Mà vaglia dir il vero nell'infinità de'cantanti celebrati da primi secoli sino à giorni nostri come gl'Orfei, gl'Anfioni, i Filamoni, gli Ardali, i Tritei, & altri, li quali per la loro innumerabilità si tralasciano, hebbero dal Cielo qualche modo musico singolare per muouere qualche particolar affetto ne petti de' mortali: Solo Claudio (stimo per fatalità così nomato chiudendosi in lui tanto valore) godè la communanza dell'affettioni e partorì à suo beneplacito nelle menti humane le dispositioni, e muoue i sensi all'elettione di quel diletto, che loro propose. Non mi lasciano mentire le moltiplici sue compositioni, ne quali hauendo compartiti i sopranominati modi, non può chi piega à quelli l'orecchio non arrendersi. Chi hà forza di rattener le lagrime, mentre s'arresta à sentir il giusto lamento dell' Infelice Ariana? Qual gioia non proua al canto de'suoi Madrigali, e composti scherzi? Forse non s'appiglia ad'vna vera deuotione chi ascolta le di lui sagre compositioni? Non si dispone ad ogni più composto viuere, chi si trattiene à goder coll'orecchio i suoi morali? E nella varietà de'suoi componimenti per cagione de Nozze de Prencipi, e ne Theatri di questa Serenissima Città rappresentati, non variano di momento in momento gl'affetti? Perche hora t'inuitano al riso, il quale in vn tratto sforzato sei cangiar in pianto, e quando pensi di pigliar l'armi alla Vendetta, all'hora appunto con miracolosa metamorfosi cangiandosi l'armonia si dispone il tuo cuore alla Clemenza: in vn subito ti senti riempire di timore, quando con altretanta fretta t'assiste ogni confidenza. Dite pur, e credetelo, Signori, che siano Apollo, e tutte le Muse concorse ad aggrandire l'eccellenza dell'ingegno di Claudio: perche Clio gl'insegnò à cantar le Vittorie, Melpomene i tragici auuenimenti; Thalia i lascini Amori, Euterpe ad accompagnar il canto con la dolcezza de' flauti. Tersicore ad aggrandire, e muouere gl'affetti. Erato à maneggiar il Plettro, Calliope à compor l'heroiche materie, Vrania ad emular i orbi celesti, Polihinnia à misurar i tempi, e finalmente Apollo quasi Maestro insegnolli l'assistere con ordine infallibile à tanta moltiplicità

cità d'officij. Era gionto all'età virile Claudio il Monte verde, e
per le singolarissime sue qualità, e dottrina era da tutti i Prencipi
desiderata, e ricercata la sua opera, mentre il Cielo per straddarlo à
maggior perfettione lo priuò della Moglie, la quale non tentò à
guisa di nouello Orfeo col suono della sua viola, di cui non hebbe
pari, richiamarla al mondo conoscendo, come fedelissimo Cattoli-
co, che gloriosa collà nel Cielo mercè alle sue sante operationi, e diuine virtù godeua quell'armonia celeste, doue con sempiterno contento fruiscono l'anime beate la visione vera del supremo bene Id-
dio. Io lasciò costei arrichito di due figliuoli, l'vno de'quali chia-
mato Francesco, consecrato alla Musica quali humanato Vsignolo
hor troncando la voce, taluolta ripigliandola, hor col fermarla, e
torcerla, ben spesso col farla piena, o scema, hor graue, hor sottile
forma vn'ampia catena de dolcissimi passaggi, con si fatto artificio
in somma ci canta, che posta gl'huomeni in obliuione ogn'altra fa-
cenda, vscendo di se stessi ammirano l'armonioso articolar del di lui
canto: L'altro detto Massimiliano, emulando Apollo l'applicò, come pur fece questi Esculapio alla Medicina : acciò se l'vno col canto alleggierisce à mortali l'angosciose cure, l'altro col ridonarle la
sanità, gl'assicurasse di vita. O' felicissimo Claudio, che più ti resta
desiderare, quando de'parti tuoi, de'tuoi figliuoli scorgi vna tal riuscita, che nati à beneficio de gl'huomeni siano da tutti acclamati, nè
lingua alcuna si muoua, che per lodarli? A questo segno erano le
glorie di Claudio, quando oltre moltissime Virtù de quali viueua
adorno era à parte d'vna somma prudenza, e pensando all'inconstan-
za della Fortuna, e che le felicità mondane per lo più terminano con
intausto fine deliberò di ricourarsi in porto sicuro da qual si uoglia
nautragio. Onde vacando in quello tempo la Ducale di S.Marco di
Maestro di Capella stimando ciò proportionato premio alla sua
Virtù, quando da quei Sauijssimi Padri fosse stato eletto à tal carica
cimentando ogni faticosa proua, elesse l'applicarsi al seruitio della
Serenissima Republica di Venetia, nel seruir la quale stimaua eleg-
gersi il proprio suo centro. Sortì non per sorte; mà per proprij meriti il gouerno di questo più celebrato Choro d'Italia, fù à pieni voti
assonto alla desiata carica, nella quale non perdonando à fatica aperse con facilità la strada alla non più vsitata forma di cantare, e sco-
stossi dall'antico rito, obligandosi però colla gentilezza de costumi
le volentà de va'orosi cantanti, i quali di buona voglia s'arresero
nel

nel abbracciare le più da loro non pratticate forme di canto. E benche fosse straniere, e d'altra Patria; nondimeno non sò, se per la co-
stanza delle Deità in fauorirlo, ò più tosto di quella de Cieli, e delle stelle in donarlo al Mondo così ripieno della vera cognitione di
questa eccellente disciplina, congiurarono tutti à suo fauore di sempre amarlo, e riuerirlo. Che però studiando con ogni spirito di cor-
rispondere al commando de suoi cenni, egli non ingrato à tanto
ossequio procuraua d'arrichirli con marauigliosa abbondanza de
modi armonici, li quali per la corrottione dell'arte erano già occulti. Seruiua con animo lieto questo Sereniſſimo Dominio solendo
dire, che per giongere alla vera, e totale perfettione della Musicale
disciplina, non poteua il Cielo collocarlo in loco, doue le cose fosse-
rò più armoniose, Considerando che questo Aristocratico gouerno
di questa Sereniſſima Republica rappresenta quel concento appunto, che vogliono le schole de' Filosofanti causarsi dall'incessante mo-
to di quei superni giri, che dalla loro Intelligenza sempiternamente
girati con non intera armonia conseruano questo inferiore globo,
stanza de noi mortali. Sconuiene forse il raffigurarsi per Ferma-
mento di questo Impero la radunanza di tante Illustriſſime Fami-
glie, le quali quasi lucidiſſime stelle cagionano benigni, e fortunati
influſſi negl' habitanti questo picciol Mondo? Il primo Mobile
non si può dir che sia il Gran Consiglio, dalla cui independente auttorità pende ogn'altro ordine, che miri all'vniuersale conseruatio-
ne? Che vogliamo chiamar l'inuiolabil Conseglio de Dieci, che
Saturno cagionante col rigido, giusto però suo seggio, infallibile
l'ordine di tutti gl'altri Magistrati inferiori. Non merita d'esser
detto Mercurio l'eccesso Colleggio, doue soggiorna l'eloquenza, e
finalmente non ruotano Marte, e Gioue entro il Senato Sacrosanto
deriuando da questo gl'influſſi di Guerra, e Pace: Sfere già tanti secoli così ben regolate, che doue la quantità de circoli con variationi
de giri dimostra confusione, e disordine, in questi apponto regolati
errori mantiene, e sempre manterrà perpetua la sua Duratione questo Sereniſſimo Dominio. In questa Città al seruitio della Ducale
Capella di S. Marco deliberò fermarsi il nostro Claudio; nostro di-
co, per hauer renontiata ogn'altra Patria; conoscendo come vero
Sauio, che doue ben si viue, quiui sia la vera Patria. Paſſarono ben
quatro lustri, che 'l Monte verde coll'animo suo riuolto alli soli stu-
dij dell'arte sua emulando ogni nuoua inuentione per l'esquilitezza

B   del

dal fuo ingegno, publicamente fù acclamato per il primo compositore conosciuto ne noſtri secoli. Non inſuperbì ad vna tanta gloria: mà ſi come col numero armonico haueua ritrouata l'arte più che perfetta della muſical compoſitione, procurò nell'auanzo de' ſuoi ſtudij auanzarſi ancora nelle Virtù non hauendo nel longo ſpatio di vinti anni intieri dato ſaggio, che di prudente, e ſauio, e ſopra'l tutto di Religioſo conſiderado, che ſe gradatamente haueua fatto sì nobil acquiſto d'eſſer glorioſo al Mondo, voleua parimente per via d'auanzati gradi ſtraddarſi alla gloria del Cielo; e perche col mezo dell' arte era già nominato diuino, volle per via dell'ordine ſacro da douero diuinizarſi. Che per tanto depoſto l'habito ſecolare veſtì l'Eccleſiaſtico, e ſi fece Sacerdote. Entri qui pur nouua pomma à deſcriuere l'integrità della ſua vita, l'eſſemplarità de ſuoi coſtumi, che non mi reſta che dire ſolo, che alla diuina vocatione diuinamente operando ſempre corriſpoſe, e dopo l'hauer con ogni ſua maggior lode vinta l'inuidia ordinaria perſecutrice di chi ſi ſtradda al ſommo della Virtù, due altri luſtri permiſe il Cielo, che Claudio Sacerdote praticando tutte le Religioſe conditioni, mà più d'ogn'altra il zelo di giouar al proſſimo datoſi alla Filoſoſia ſoſſe dietro alla compoſitione d'vn volume, nelquale notificando i più occulti arcani della ſua diſciplina era per impedire, che mai più ne ſecoli venturi reſtaſſero naſcolte à ſtudenti le vere ſtradde per facilitarſi l'acquiſto della perfettione dell'arte Muſica. Mà l'empia morte affrettata da breue intermità hà cagionato, che come imperfetta reſti priua della luce della ſtampa. Hà però colle fatiche ſue operato viuendo, che ſe ne tempi andati ſi valeuano i Padri preſtantiſſimi de Foreſtieri, e conduceuano al loro ſeruitio muſici alienigeni, tale, e tanto ſia conoſciuto il profitto de ſuoi documenti, che la Città di Venetia abbondando de ſingolariſſimi ingegni, li quali in tal profeſſione col di lui aiuto altamente profondano, può arrichir di queſti li più famoſi, e celebri Chori d'Europa ſenza impouerir ſe ſteſſa. In queſto ſtato ſi ritrouaua Claudio Monte verde, quando non sò con buona licenza degl'Illuſtriſſimi, & Eccellentiſſimi Procuratori di Chieſa di S. Marco mettoſi à peregrinare la Lombardia nel ſpatio di meſi ſei riuidde, e fauorì colla ſua preſenza le già da lui fauorite Città, che deſioſe di rimirarlo attendeuano occaſione di ſignificarle con lieti incontri quanto ſtimauano la di lui virtù: mà eſſendo homai vecchio, e cadente nell'eceſſo di tante honoratiſſime accoglienze ſoprafatto da

vna

vna stravagante debolezza di Forze, maggiormente però avalorandosi nell'animo presaggi à se medesimo in età così grave l'vltimo accidente, & à guisa di Cigno, che presentendo l'hora fatale de' suoi giorni s'auuicina all'acque, e dentro di esse formando con più soaue armonia del solito dolcissimi passaggi passa il Musico Gentile all'altra vita: Così Claudio ritornò volando non nell'acque di Meandro: mà nelle più fauorite dell'Adriatico Scilo, doue la marauiglia risedendo è necessitato chi s'approssima ammirar gl'eccessi della natura, e dell'arte; ritornò volando à Venetia Regina dell'acque e figlia di Nettuno, doue oltre la Brenta, l'Adige, il Sil, la Liuenza corre ancora come Tributario à riuerirla con arena d'oro il Vastissimo Eridano. Giunto alle desiate acque l'humanato Cigno ricercò colla delicatezza solita d'armoniosi componimenti la riueduta Patria, aggrauato però dal settuagesimoquinto anno con breue intermità, e poca per hauer poco del Terrestre, armato de Sagramenti Ecclesiastici desideroso d'andar collà tra Serafini lasciò la spoglia mortale, ed vnissi con Dio.

La nuoua di tanta perdita turbò, e rese tutta la Città mesta, & addolorata, e tù dal Choro de Cantori accompagnata non con canto, mà con lagrime, e pianto, sopramodo deuoti del suo nome, & ossequiosi à suoi cenni: mà considerando, che cangiato di terreno in celeste Cigno doueua sonrattanto tra Cherubini armoniose, e diuine melodie, deposta ogni tristezza deliberarono tutti concordi honorarlo d'vno de più solenni funerali, che reduti, & vditi haubi la Patria regolato dal Molto Illustre Signor Giouanni Rouetta, che conosciuto il più valoroso d'ogn'altro, emulo del defonto essercita la già vacata carica, & à gran passi coll'altezza de suoi componimenti arriuato ad ogni maggior perfettione rà di se medesimo formar concetti di miracolosa riuscita. Non contento però di quello benchè grandissimo honore l'animo del Molto Illustre, e Molto Reuerendo Signor D. Gio: Battista Marinoni cognominato Gione, come grauido d'ogni maggior dimostratione di gratitudine per li riceuuti beneficij da vn'huomo di tanto merito, pochi giorni doppo con pompa veramente regia eretto vn Catafalco nella Chiesa de Padri Minori de Frari vestita tutta di bruno; mà rassembrante vna lucidissima notte ricca d'infinite stelle per il gran numero d'accesi lumi; deliberò di far celebrar vn nuouo funerale dalui regolato con vna dimostratione del valor suo, che in rego-

B 2

lindo il più numeroso choro, che far potesse la Città, ne riportò di
Peritissimo Maestro il nome. Tali sono, ò Signori, i Guadagni auan-
taggioli di chi viuendo mercantino la Virtù. Vorrei più oltre se-
guire, o Claudio il racconto de tuoi alti meriti per le tue non ordi-
narie prerogatiue: mà sentendomi collà dal Cielo sgridar
la mia debolezza più tosto scemante, che dimo-
strante l'altezza tua. Quindi deuotissimo al nome tuo m'in-
chino, e più
che
volonteroso, e pieno di ossequio mi taccio.
* t. *

IN LAVDEM

PERILLVSTRIS, ET ADMODVM REVERENDI

D. CLAVDM MONDIS VIRIDIS

IN VENETIARVM DIVI MARCI BASILICA

MVSICORVM PRAEFECTI EXCELLENTISSIMI

HEXASTICON

MATTHAEI CABERLOTI.
PLEBANI S. THOMAE.

Montis in excelso placuit celare Tonanti
  Semina Virtutum vel potiora Iugu

Cælius inclusam sophiam iam reddidit; ortum,
  Carmina traxerunt ex Helicone prius

At si quem Musicę delectet, Claudius iste
  Mons Viridis numeros, signa, modosq: dedit.

IN MORTE

DEL SIGNOR CLAVDIO MONTEVERDE

MAESTRO DI CAPELLA

DELLA SERENISSIMA SIGNORIA,
Il maggior Musico di Europa:

DEL PADRE MAESTRO PAVLO PIAZZA.

Al fiero suon di furibondo Marte,
   Scomposta è ogni Armonia, roca ogni tromba,
   Di barbarici accenti, il ciel ribomba
   Del fiume altero l'vna, e l'altra parte.

Non più i cigni, d'Amor spiegano l'arte,
   V' bellica bombarda ogn'hora fiomba,
   Ben di mille Fetonti fate Tomba,
   Vergano hor d'ire le fluttuose carte.

Chiusero Claudio, e Numa il sacro Tempio
   Ch'hoggi barbara man apre, e disserra
   Con barbaro furor profano, ed empio.

S'hor chiuso è Claudio, è'l Armonia sotterra
   Meraviglia non fia; che al crudo scempio
   Cadono i Plettri, e le sampogne in Terra.

IN

IN MORTE
DELL'ECCELLENTISSIMO
SIGNOR CLAVDIO
MONTEVERDE.

ALLA MORTE.

Aspra ben cruda farce
   Quanto, quanto sospiro
   Se ti contemplo, ohime se ti rimiro
   Tu, c'hai rapito il Canto
   Di Monte Verde il Vanto,
   Perfida, e spietata
   Alla Virtude ingrata
   Ah, ch'all'Imperio tuo nulla s'ascriue
   s'estinto giace, l'opra sua s'en viue,

DEL

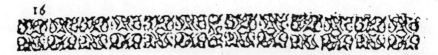

DEL REVERENDISSIMO
DON PIETRO QVADRARIO,
PIOVAN IN S. GIACOMO
DALL'ORIO.

⁎⁎*⁎*

Ninfe del bel permeſſo
    Scapigliate correte à l'alta Pirà.
    Caduto oue ſi mira
    Il MONTE VERDE voſtro, aridi i fiori:
    Coſi à le Faci acceſe, à tanti ardori,
    Al lacrimare amaro,
    Foſſe quà giù conceſſo
    Auuiuar il ſuo nome illuſtre, e chiaro;
    Mà, che dico auuiuar CLAVDIO co'l pianto?
    Che ſe da noi ſi parte
    Ancor, ch'eſtinto, viue in le ſue Carte.

IN

IN INSIGNI FVNERALIVM CELEBRITATE

Perilluſtris, & Admodum Reucrendi Domini

CLAVDII MONTEVERDIS

IN SACRA DIVI MARCI VENETIARVM AEDE
Muſicorum Prefeĉti.

Dialogiſmus.

Hoſpes   &   Poeta.

EPYGRAMMA.

H. Quis cętus Populi? P. Populi plorantis. H. & vndè?
P. Expediunt funĉto funera mæſta Viro.

H. Dic mihi, quis periit? P. neſcis? H. non. P. CLAVDIVS ille
MONSVIRIDIS diĉtus, Muſica dona dicans.

H. Quando agè, dic, periit? P. nunquam, ſed viuere cœpit
Quando mori eſt viſus, Morsquè ità Vita fuit.

H. Viuit adhuc ergo? P. melius, quàm vixerit ante.
H. Cum quo? P. cum Chr.ſto, deſuper Aſtra P.li.

H. Fœlix, quem funĉtum Populi lacrymantur: P. Olympo
Cui poſita eſt Mercces, Gloria, Vita, Quies.

Fr. Maur. Monc. Fer. Min. Con.

C   IN

IN OBITV, ET FVNERE EIVSDEM

CLAVDII MONTEVERDIS

Infignis Muficalium Moderatoris.

MODVLATORES AD ILLIVS ANIMAM.

ECHO.

EPYGRAMMA.

Quò abis, ò CLAVDI, Mundo renocante ?　E. *vocante.*
　Quòne, vocante fugis ? vel nece, vel Deo?　E. *eo.*

Curnè Deus nolit Mundo te linquere ?　　E. *quære.*
　Quæram: fortè cares diuitijs ?　　　E. *vitijs.*

Magna carens vitijs Virtus vult viuere.　E. *verè.*
　Vitane dat verè viuere perdita?　　E. *ità.*

Mors hæc non eft Mors, quia viuere redditur.　E. *itur.*
　Iturnè, vt viuas, non moriens?　　E. *oriens.*

Vita tua hæc oriens Superis redamatur ?　E. *amatur.*
　In Cælis nunquam Gloria deerit?　　E. *erit.*

Dant Regi Regum Regalia munera Reges,
　Muficus ipfe dabis Mufica tu Deo.　　E. *eo.*

Eiufdem Authoris.

NEL

NEL FVNERALE DELL'ECCELLENTISSIMO DOTTOR
MONTE VERDE
MAESTRO DI CAPELLA DI S. MARCO,
DI VENETIA:

FATTO DAL MOLTO REVERENDO
SIG. DON GIO: BATTISTA MARINONI,
Detto Gioue, in Venetia.

DI D. ALFONSO GRILOTTI,
Cognominato Targa, nobile Vrbinate.

Cruda Morte n' eſtinſe il vaſto Aloro
   Che di Parnaſo diede il biondo Dio,
   Ma non fia ſua virtù vada in oblio
   Nè, che perdan le Muſe il lor decoro.

Mira come dal Ciel vn nuouo choro
   Gioue ne fà ſentir il ſuo deſio
   Dicendo ſe morì, non già morio
   Delli Arcani di quel il gran teſoro.

Noi, che tutto regiam, Parnaſo ancora
   Farem, che reſta in terra il Verde Monte
   Ne tempo ne ſtagion il diſcolora.

Coſì contra la morte, il tempo, e l'onte
   Conuerrà il ſuo valor ſi ſenta, e honora
   Sin oue il Sol fa 'l gir all' Orizonte.
                 C 2   CIAV-

CLAVDIO MONTE VERDE
ANAGRAMMA
CVORE D'ALMA DIVENTO.
DI ANTONIO DI VESCOVI.

Per maggioranza hauere tra' mortali
   T'Appigli al Monte, c'hà fentiero al Cielo
   Le margherite fan pretiofo gelo
   Nelle Valli del Monte, e fuoi Canali

Nel ventre fon rinchiufi tanti, e tali
   Metalli, che à gli abiffi ftan per velo
   La Cima, e tutta Verde à pelo à pelo
   Con piante, fiori, e frutti anche Immortali.

Da quefta altezza paffi alla fublime
   Nell'vna, e l'altra melodia, e contento
   Godi, con rauuinar l'eccelfi Rime.

Mentr'io, ch'all'harmonia tua ftauo inuento
   Nomino tue Virtù, benche le prime
   CVORE D'ALME gioconde à pien DIVENTO.

IN

IN MORTE DI CLAVD!O

MONTE VERDE:

MAESTRO DI MVSICA
Il più celebre del noftro fecolo.

****

In funebri Cipreffi, in fcuri Acanti,
Cangi i Lauri il Caftalio, e l'Ippocrene,
Amphione, Orpheo, i Cigni, e le Sirene
Volgano i Canti, e i fuoni in trifti pianti;

Fugan le Mufe fconfolate erranti
Gli horti d'Apollo, e le contrade amene,
Piangan le Regie, gemano le Scene,
Sian le Lire, e le Cetre orbe vaganti.

Morto è colui, che a Numeri fonori,
Pieni di foauiffima dolcezza,
I mutoli Theatri fea canori.

Morto è colui, che rider la Triftezza
Facea nel pianto, e ne'ridenti chori
Inconfolabil pianger l'Allegrezza.

P. P.

I N

IN MORTE

DI CLAVDIO MONTEVERDE,

Gran professor della Chimica.

DEL PADRE MAESTRO
PAVLO PIAZZA.

Mura fallace, lusinghiera, e vana,
   Che d'hauer, di saper sempre il cor ange,
   Qual mai riempie ne l'aurato Gange,
   Ne di chimico Argento Arte profana;

Insaciabile rea voglia mondana,
   Ch'el certo bene, per l'incerto infrange,
   Ne perche vegga ogn'hor, ch'el vento frange,
   Lascia, anzi accresce d'ogni industria humana;

Claudio, se chiude, gl'occhi, apre l'ingegno,
   Esperto hormai ch'vn soffio toglie, e fura,
   Ad'Anima Gentil Preggio condegno;

Là s'alza oue Ricchezza eterna dura,
   Che ben dà d'arricchir sicuro pegno,
   Città ch'hà d'or le Piazze, e d'or le Mura.

IN

180

IN MORTE
DI CLAVDIO MONTE VERDE,
MAESTRO DI CAPELLA
IN S. MARCO.

CLAVDIO nacque all' impero, onde al confine,
    Stese dell' vniuerso il scetro aurato ,
    Trionfante la fama, al mar gelato,
    Portò suoi preggi, perche à lui s'inchine .

MONTE ameno, e giocondo il folto crine
    Nutre con puro fonte albergo grato ,
    Dal biondo Dio dalle Pimpliadi amato
    Forma, e comparte sue magion diuine .

VERDE trattien l'Alloro il sacro manto,
    Così la Palma vnita al proprio stelo,
    Ambi danno à Virtude il maggior vanto .

CLAVDIO imperò trà Cigni in mortal velo:
MONTE fù delle Muse; erge al suo canto
VERDE Alloro la Terra, e Palme il Cielo .

IN

IN MORTE
DEL SIGNOR CLAVDIO
MONTE VERDE,
MAESTRO DI CAPELLA IN S. MARCO DI VENETIA.

Inuida Morte se ti lodi, e vanti
  Del Colpo, ch'atterò l' huom sacro à Dio
  Scoprendo contro lui empio 'l desio
  Che la vita menò con dolci Canti.

Rallegrati Signor, che fuor di pianti
  Da te stess. sparisti, e in dolce riso
  Gode quel'armonia del Paradiso
  L'vnica tua Virtù nel lume santo.

Ti fa l'essequie Apollo, e in graue passo
  Meste ti seguon le canore Dine
  E tutto pindo addolorato, e lasso

Indi con piuma d'or in suon più basso
  Queste notte d'honor la gloria scriue
  Qui giace Claudio chiuso in questo sasso.

IN

IN LODE DEL MOLTO ILLVSTRE,
ET MOLTO REVERENDO
SIGNOR DON GIO:BATTISTA MARINONI
DETTO GIOVE:
PER IL FVNERALE
FATTO Al MOLTO ILLVSTRE, & ECCELLENTISSIMO
MAESTRO DI CAPELLA
DI S. MARCO DI VENETIA
CLAVDIO MONTEVERDE.

DI D. ALFONSO GRILLOTTI,
Cognominato Targa, nobile Vrbinato.

Delli Abiffi il decor de tanto i canti
   Sparfe d'honor quel, che l'honor fi preme
   E 'l fin altro non fù, nè fù altra fpeme
   Sol, che di Claudio rauuiuar i vanti.

Ond' alli Frari fi diuerfi, e tanti,
   Fece Gioue fentir vniti infieme,
   Morienti Cigni, e come il lutto freme,
   Trà funebri apparati Organ tremanti.

Nella Vergin intatta il grido fparfo,
   Chi di fcienza è pien di faper carco
   Per mirar', e gradir, ne venne al Tempio.

Cofi d'amor reftò quafi il cor arfo
   Del Mariner le proue à Pietro, e Marco
   Ch'effaltan la Virtù fotterran l'empio.

               D   IN

IN MORTE
DELL' ECCELLENTISSIMO
MONTE VERDE:

MADRIGALE:

Gloria à Dio, Pace all' Huom, Musici egreggi
   Debbon spiegar canori,
   Nel vicino Natal del Rè de Regi.
   Faran la Terra, e 'l Ciel l'ampio Theatro,
   Stupiran Tile, e Battro,
   A i dolcissimi accenti de Cantori.
   CLAVDIO gran MASTRO della melodia,
   Composta hà l'armonia.
   Mà, da Barbara Guerra
   Vietato ci d'annuntiar la Pace in Terra.
   (Il suo Mortal conquiso)
   Gito e a Cantar la Gloria in Paradiso.

P. P.

NEL

NELLA MORTE

DELL'ECCELLENTISSIMO SIGNOR

CLAVDIO MONTEVERDE.

DI DON ALFONSO GRILOTTI,
Cognominato Targa, Nobil Vrbinato.

Tù, che dal Ciel in Terra eletto fosti
    Anima, à far perfetto il canto e 'l suono
    Dopo hauer col saper moſtrato il dono,
    Furno gli organi tuoi franti, e depoſti.

La Morte, e 'l Tempo vniti, e ben diſpoſti
    Come ſoglian oprar, ſenza perdono
    Penſando (il corpo gia giacendo pronto)
    Far come pria, e laſciar quei ſcompoſti.

Ma doue il gran Signor opra, e diſpone
    Il peſſimo penſier luogo non troua
    Nè può far di Virtù l'obliuione.

Onde ſia mentre 'l ver, e il ſol ſi troua,
    Delle ſcienze tue dotto Campione
    Vna eterna memoria, e ſempre noua.

D 2   IN

IN MORTE
DEL FAMOSISSIMO
MONTE VERDE.

Pindo, non è più Pindo, il Lauro è secco,
   Apollo fosco, e le Pierie mute
   Piangon le Glorie loro (Ahime) perdute.
   E conuerso in horrore
   Di Parnaso l' Honore
   Per le fiorite arene
   Non più corre Hippocrene;
   E 'l celebre Pegaso
   Abbandona d' humori esausto il Vaso:
   Pindo non è più Pindo. Hoggi si perde:
   Non più haurà Apollo, il caro Monte Verde.

P.

ALLE

ALLE MVSE DE NOSTRI TEMPI:

MADRIGALE

DI DON AMBROSIO ROSSI:

O' voi, che d' Ippocrene al sacro fonte
  E d' Elicona ad' habitar il Monte
  Volgiete il piede
  E fretoloso il passo
  Ritardate il voler, che già rissiede
  In quest' orrido sasso
  Del Musico sapere il ditto Apollo
  Cessi pur d: Talia Comico il Canto
  E d' Euterpe il saper, L'Erato il vanto.
  Tersicore con Clio
  Calliope con Pollinnia
  Melpomene, ed' Vrania, al parer mio,
  Potran solo col gesto
  Spiegar i loro accenti
  Se morto giace, chi li dia la Voce.

IE

LE MVSE,
IN RISPOSTA DELL' ANTECEDENTE
MADRIGALE:
DELL' ISTESSO.

Se giace in quesla Tomba Apollo il sacro
   Da cui era la voce di noi Muse
   Con vero modo
   E con perfetto nodo
   Concatenata, e giuslamente retta
   Non ti prender slupore
   Che se mancato ci è
   Dal Padre natural Febo il calore.
   Commiserando à nostri prieghi il sommo
   Ci è degnato qui giù discender Giove.

ALLA

ALLA MORTE DELL'ECCELLENTISSIMO SIGNOR CLAVDIO MONTE VERDE.

DEL PADRE BAC. SIMON OLMO. MIN. CON.

Giace trà pietre il Monte,
  Che di musici applausi il preggio ottenne,
  Giace quì ; ma d'Apollo al sacro fonte,
  Sempre viuran del suo valor le penne ;
  E giusto, e ben, che se d'eterno amore
  Con sue voci Canore,
  Già noi mortali accese,
  Hor d'insigne Vittoria,
  Goda Cigno sublime eterna Gloria.

ALL'ISTESSO.

Verdeggiante Corone al Verde Monte
  Cingasi hoggi d'Allori
  Toi ch'alla meta de sublimi honori
  Hà posto il piè con vittoriosa fronte ;
  Ergasi vn bel Trofeo d'accenti e Carmi
  E si regga destino
  Qui giace il Monte Glorioso estinto.

I N

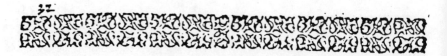

IN MORTE
DEL SIGNOR CLAVDIO
MONTE VERDE:

Da questi chiostri parte
   Canoro sì, ma imparigiabil Cigno
   Mansueto, e benigno
   Messaggiero s' en uia
   Per la Celeste via
   Scende volando al Cielo
   Per impetrar da quello
   Con sue note gentil vera, e verace
   All'esito fatal d'Italia pace.

IN

IN MORTE DI D. CLAVDIO
MONTE VERDE.

CONTRAPVNTO POETICO.

Note confuse , Parti sconcertate ,
  Aspre soauità , dolcezze amare ,
  Suon dissuonante , vnisono dispare ,
  Mutole Voci , non articolate ;

Musiche meste , allegre , sconsolate ,
  Soaui crudità , concento impare ,
  Rotti ragiri , roco gorgheggiare ,
  Cetre , Viole , à tuono discordate ;

Lugubri Melodie , Flebili accenti ,
  Passaggi torti , canti lacrimosi ,
  S'odano mormorar sordi stromenti

Apollo è morto , il Dio degli Armoniosi ,
  Rissuonino le lingue , l'Aure , e i Venti ,
  Cromatici sospiri , Dolorosi .

P. P.

E IN

191

IN MORTE
DELL'ECCELLENTISSIMO
SIGNOR CLAVDIO
MONTE VERDE.

Claudio? chiuso sei quì? Morto nò. Viui
Io piangendo ti piango al Ciel Canoro
Non moristi tù già : Ma viui ai Diui
A i Diui spirti del Celeste Choro.

Tu di dolor la mente mia ci priui
Ch' io per Legiaco Cantor tue Glorie honoro
Con il pianto funereo , il quale auuiui
Con il plettro Immortal , ch' io piango, e adoro.

Horrida Morte à te troncò la Vita
Per farsi anch' essa Musica al tuo Canto
Ond' io piango per te Morte Tradita.

Anzi per inalzarti al Cielo ; hai vanto
Di superar la Morte in te rapita
Perdoni al Canto mio Glorioso il pianto.

IN.

192

IN MORTE

DEL SIGNOR DON CLAVDIO

MONTE VERDE

FRA OTTAVIO RAGVCCI
Maeſtro di Studio nel Collegio di Padoua Min. Con.

****

Poſero già , per mouer al Ciel guerra ,
  Forſenati Giganti , con lor poſſa ,
  L'vn ſopra l'altro Pelio , Olimpo , & Oſſa ,
  Monti , più ſmiſurati della terra.

Ma chi all'empireo , commanda , & imperra
  Non ſoffrì già , la temeraria moſſa ,
  Ma ſuiſcerò , ne monti , e tomba , e foſſa
  Oue l'ardir ſuperbo ſi rinſerra .

Ecco nouo portento , l'armonia
  Per ripor il ſuo ſeggio , in Paradiſo ,
  Nel MONTE VERDE , inueſtigar la via ;

Di lui ſcala ſi fa , da noi ſi ſcioglie ,
  Con CLAVDIO parte , e ſe con meſto viſo ,
  La piange il Mondo , lieto il Ciel l'accoglie .

E   NEL-

NELLA MORTE
DELL'ECCELLENTISSIMO CLAVDIO
MONTE VERDE.

DI DON ALFONSO GRILOTTI,
Cognominato Targa, Nobil Vrbinate.

Non si dolgan viuenti,
   S'estinto in Terra giace,
   E' membri in polue sface,
   L'Amato Monte verde,
   Che la morte vincendo, egli non perde;
   Poi, che canto Materno
   Cambiò col ver' eterno.
   E dall'onde la Regia
   Lasciò, per goder quel, che più si pregia.

DEL

DEL PADRE MAESTRO ANTONIO ADAMI

LOGICO PVBLICO DI PADOVA.

L' empireo è vn monte, & è la Gloria vn verde
　　Stabile è quello, e sempre viva, è questa
　　Iui non giunge fulmine ò Tempesta
　　E posseduta, poi mai non si perde

La Fama vola mà non si disperde
　　Che con il tronco della gloria inesta
　　Non cede al Tempo; e l'ali non arresta
　　Il Compendio del Cielo, è il Monte verde .

Ti tolse il faro ò Claudio : e pur sei vivo
　　Che in Cielo regni ; è in Terra anco immortale
　　Non muore il Verde è sol di vita privo .

Che se da cupa ò da profonda vale
　　Rimira il Cielo Huomo Celeste ò Diuo
　　Lo tira à se, Ch' è di natura tale .

DEL

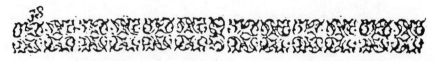

DEL PADRE MAESTRO ANTONIO ADAMI

LOGICO PVBLICO DI PADOVA.

Del Cielo sregolato era il concento
    Rapido il corso de Pianetti, e Stelle,
    E senza tempo il tempo d questi ò quelle
    Donaua il moto hora veloce, hor lento .

La pausa agl'elementi, era vn portento
    E s'vdia da mortali alte querele
    Noui motti, noue ombre, arme nouelle,
·   Onde il Mondo al finir pareua intento .

Che s'aspetta ò mortali d che si attende
    Chi le misure, e i numeri comparte
    Chi le note distingue ò i Tempi intende .

Lasci (fia, meglio) di vergar le carte
    Che ad'altro regno il suo valor s'estende
    E regoli del Ciel l'vltima parte.

PER

PER IL SIGNOR MONTE
VERDE.

Per terminar, à chi si deue il pregio
  Di musico diuin, co'l santo choro
  Delle Muse, il bel Dio dai raggi d'oro
  S'vnì nel beatissimo Collegio.

Dierno lor voti al fine, ch'all'egregio
  Gran *MONTE VERDE*, qual io tanto onoro,
  Fosser date le chiaui del tesoro,
  Sopra cui gli suoi pari han priuilegio.

Per diuina sentenza: tu, che sei
  Dunque de i tuoi simili il più facondo,
  (Guai, chi al giuditio s'oppon degli Dei)

Celebrato sarai per tutto il Mondo,
  O' degno fior di tutti i semidei,
  Non sol per primo, ma senza secondo.

G. A. N. A.

CLAV.

CLAVDIO MONTEVERDE:
ANAGRAMMA
DOVE NEL CVOR MEDITA:
DE ANTONIO DE VESCOVI.

* * * * *

La Mufica reggeua Claudio in Terra,
    Naturale, & humana,
    L'artificiale ancor, che non, è ftrana;
    Ma Theorica con pratica, in fe ferra
Contiene la vocale,
Di più l'inftromentale,
Diuife in regolare, e irregolare,
La figurale, e mifurale in tutto,
Guidaua con gran frutto;
Già è andato à gouernare
La Mufica celefte: e Gioue il loda,
Lo MEDITA NEL CVOR DOVE più goda.

IN

IN MORTE DI CLAVDIO MONTE VERDE:

DI DON ALFONSO GRILOTTI,
Cognominato Targa, Nobil Vrbinate.

Dolor, che preme il petto, e l'Alma afferra,
　Nel sentir, che la Morte il colpo crudo,
　Tirò per annullar il forte scudo,
　Del Verde Monte, e lo mandò sotterra,

Pianga pur Elicona, e grida, e sferra,
　Ogn' allegrezza, hor, ch' il suo Monte, e ignudo,
　Non potendo più dir in quel racchiudo,
　La speme del tuo honor in ond', e 'n Terra.

Lacrimando le Muse Apollo intanto,
　Volò nell'alto Ciel, e pregò Gioue,
　Facesse del estinto eterno il vanto.

Gratiò dicendo non son Muse noue
　Rinuerda dunque il Monte, e non più il piano
　Decima questa sia mia mente moue
　　　　　　　　Così sue Gratie Pioue

A chi delle Virtù passa viuenti
　S' inchinò Apollo, e diede i vani à Venti
Rallegrando Parnaso, Fonte, e Sore
　Cantard'l nome ou'egli sorge, e more.

　　　　　F　　　NEL-

NELLA MORTE
DELL'ECCELLENTISSIMO CLAVDIO
MONTE VERDE.

Com'hai tù Parca ria lo flame incifo
   Di Claudio Monte Verde heroe pietofo,
   Anzi Immortal frà noi Padre amorofo,
   E feco di mill'Alme il Ciel recifo.

Com'hai di Delo il Figlio à noi diuifo,
   E chiufo in duro faffo, e dolorofo,
   Oue l'offa immortal hanno ripofo,
   E l'Alma al Creator in Paradifo.

Quiui mefte le pompe, e Funerali,
   La fquilla di Parnafo alta rimbomba,
   Ou' egli nel Feretro hà i fuoi Natali.

La lira Orfeo appende à la gran Tomba,
   La fampogna Sileno, il Tempo l'Ali,
   Pallade i fuoi trofei, Fama la Tromba.

NEL-

NELLA MORTE
DEL R. SIGNOR DON CLAVDIO
MONTE VERDE.

In questa Tomba giace il Monte Verde,
  Frà mill' alti Cipressi angusta bara,
  O' Cruda ste'la, o fera Parca auara,
  Che per vederlo al Ciel, à noi si perde.

E forsi hoggi la sù doue si crede,
  Per far Musica à Gioue il Dio di Delo;
  Porta inuidia col Canto ancor nel Cielo,
  Frà gli Angeli Canor premio si vede;

Forma di Pianto ogni Theatro vn Rio,
  Mille Chori Vlular, grida Parnaso,
  La sirena del Mondo al Ciel sen' gio.

Piangono i numi d'Adria il fiero caso,
  Calpestrano le Cetre, Erato, e Clio,
  Per far al suo Signor l'vltimo occaso.

NELLA MORTE
DEL SIGNOR CLAVDIO
MONTE VERDE,

Il Primo tra' Musici.

* * * * *

Già s'è oscurato il Sole
Nella nube fatal di Morte Auara
Luce perfetta e rara
Di Musicali accenti
Nel Ciel di sua Virtù campeggia ardenti.
Già la fama è volata
Da per tutto adorata
Che viuer gioua s'è già corso il volo
Dalla Candida Aurora, al negro Polo.

NEL-

NELLA MORTE
DEL MOLTO ILLVSTRE, ET REVERENDO MONSIGNOR CLAVDIO MONTE VERDE.

DELL' ECCELLENTISSIMO SIGNOR GVERINO RODISEO.

Tinfe mufico incanto
  Nel Mondo il Monte Verde ,
  E trattò così ben voci canore ,
  Che l'armonie del Ciel s'vdiro in Terra
  Hor finfonia d'Amore
  In dolorofo Pianto
  Pompa del fuo Cantar Thalia differra
  Grida , e batte la fronte
  Ahi cade il Monte Verde, e fecco il Monte .

Dunque foggiace à morte
  Anco Monte fonoro
  Hor , che caduto à i colpi
  Accoglie il Monte Verde vn Picciol faffo
  Ah' convien, ch'io t'incolpi
  Sorte crudel, rea forte
  Ch'à quefla cieca fecondafti il paffo
  Ch' al fine al braccio afciutto
  Cedono i marmi, & obedifce il tutto .

Non

Non più la nobil vena
  Del ricco Monte-Verde
  Nella regia dell' onde.
  Porta di degno canto alto Thesoro ;
  Si disperde , e s'asconde
  Si discioglie , e si suena
  Ond'è lugubre il Palco , e muto il Choro
  Cangia il Lauro in Cipresso
  E co'l luto lo bagna il bel permesso.

Sciolte le bionde Chiome
  Il gran Pastor d'Anfriso
  A la sua Pirra intorno
  Piange il suo Cigno ad'hor, ad'hor sepolto ;
  E nel suo petto adorno
  L'angosciose some
  Sgrana tutt'hor collacrimante il Volto .
  Mentre rimira piena
  D'horror la soglia , e di dolor la scena .

Già si confonde e langue
  L'armonico concerto
  Che ne i Theatri augusto
  Fece Claudio sentir con dolci accenti ;
  Perde la Vita , e i gusti
  E il rito morto esangue
  E la pena fa rauchi i tuoi lamenti
  Co'l gran cantor, che tace
  La melodia di Cuori , estinta giace .

Dicena , e la sua Voce
  A cento lumi il lacrimar aperse
  Ahi , che non basta vn fonte
  A tornar verde , oue si secca vn Monte .

AL

AL MOLTO REVERENDO
SIGNOR DON GIO: BATTISTA
MARINONI:
NEL FVNERALE FATTO AL SIGNOR MONTE VERDE.
DI D. ALFONSO GRILLOTTI,
Cognominato Targa.

Tù, che ſi grati honori
    Fai ſentir trà gl' orrori
    A queſta Alta Regina,
    Cui Terra, e l'onde inchina,
    Del Monte verde i vanti,
    Decor de vaghe Muſe, e dotti canti ;
    Merauiglia non fia, ne coſe noue,
    Perche Perche ſei Gioue.

NEL

NELLA MORTE
DELL' ECCELLENTISSIMO
SIGNOR CLAVDIO
MONTE VERDE:

MAESTRO DI CAPELLA
DI SAN MARCO DI VENETIA.

Sospirò Apollo, e di dolor ripieno,
    Cangiò il suo sguardo; e'l rubicondo affetto.
    E di mesto color, così constretto,
    Concritio mostrossi, e non sereno.

Nel sentir, che di già il Verde e ameno
    Monte giacea estinto. Il suo diletto.
    Con vn tronco parlar, quasi imperfetto
    Disse; è morto del canto vn Dio terreno.

Le Muse in Elicona astanti al fonte.
    E'l Caual Pegaseo con duol' interno,
    Pensar passato fosse; oue è Caronte.

Ma il gran Gioue, che regge il Ciel, l'inferno;
    Tra il pianto apparue, e 'ntonò in lieta fronte.
    Viua di Claudio il nomi; viua in eterno.

Pietro Maurici.

I A.

ate

IACOBVS PIGHETTVS PATRITIVS BERGOMAS.

SVSPIRATE CHORI, LVGETE THEATRA
VESTER HONOR, GLORIA VESTRA
CLAVDIVS MONS VIRIDIS.
INCLYTVS DIVI MARCI MVSICAE PRAEFECTVS
Aeternum hic tacet, aeternum hic iacet
Eheu sic igitur con   Mons ille nobilis
Qui
Non Pegasi percultus vngulis inexhaustum praebuit fontem
Sed Charitum excultus manibus pretiosos mellite harmonie fructus
Mortalibus
Eheu sic perijt ille Diuinus
Qui
Noftrorum animorum affectus miris vfq; adeo
permulcebat concentibus,
Vt Mufas Coeleftibus Orbibus affidentes canere si quando voluerint
Doctis ipsius notis vocem emodulaturas
Iure Credideris .
Ah nimis, & vero abijt nunquam rediturus
Mulice lepos , Mel harmonie , Carminum Anima
Noftri feculi Ornamentum
Apollo fidereo detracto amictu atroq; obductus
Merore confectus auream negligat cytharam ,
Erato , Thalia , Melpomene , Futerpe , ceterea; Pierides
infolabiliter confufe
Flebilibus querelis memorabilem fateantur iacturam
Iple deniq; Aurae fuauibus tanti myxtae modis
poft hac non amplius demulcende
Trifti murmurillo fuum oftentent dolorem .
Vos autem Veneti Ciues veftro gratiffimo viduati delicio
Funus maeftiffimis lacrymis decorate .
Sufpirate Chori, Lugete Theatra .

G   O' LE-

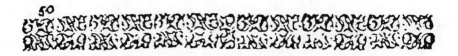

O LECTOR BENIGNE

Tempus ab antiquis tumulis sua iura reposcit
 Et clausam in lucem corpora adusta petit

Ossa iacent passim , que spirant funera mortis
 Ossa patent veram mortis in effigiem

Hospes in aspectu mesto , cur pallidus heres
 Et retrahis celeres corde tremente pedes

Siste gradum , horres quid vane simulacra figures
 Exemplum forine , quam fugis intus habes .

O MORS?

O' MORS? EHEV MORS? QVID LVGEO?

Claudius Mons Viridis obijt
  At non obijt ; sed vixit
Humanitas Immortalis .
Mirum hoc ? Hoc mirum ?
Mortalitas Diuinitùs Humana
Humanitas Humanitùs Diuina
Non extinxit ; sed euexit ad sidera Mortem
Claudium numericis lacrymis deflendum .
O' Virum Armonicis cycnis Dulcissimum .
O' Montem Viridem nunquam moriturum :
Musarum, Pieridumq; Apollo .
Melodiæ Phœbus Alter .
Cytharæ flebilis Æthereus mortalis Homo
Elegiacas sistite funeri lacrymas .
At Corpori Humanitate iam perfuncto .
Exequias funerate moni Dulcissimas
Vitæ clausit oculos Claudius, vt virtutis aperiat lumina
Non horrorè mortis, sed Virtutis Amore .
Homo Iam obijt, vt Vir semper vixeret
Viduata Virtus tanti expensa dolore funeris
Librat sanguinis officia ; Amoris consecrat fletus
Quid Claudi? Claudi quid ?
Clausit Claudius spheras Orbis iam obitu suo
Eclypticam Virtutis Mons Viridis iam tenuit
Calame tu quoq; luges ?
Non lacrimas sed Cantus dale Claudio personantes
Non perut Mortuus vt periret ; sed vixit vixus, vt vixeret
Tantus Virtutis Heros soli lumina Clausit .
Non Mirum Claudius nanq; Cælis Claudius
Sic non scripsit : sic non cecinit
At sic flexit , ac posuit Amicus .

Francisci Bolani Patritij Veneti.

G 2   DE

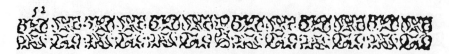

DE PRAESTANTIA

PERILLVSTRIS, ET ADM. REVERENDI

D. CLAVDII MONTIS VIRIDIS

IN ECCLESIA DIVI MARCI
VENETIARVM
MVSICORVM MAGISTRI
PRAECLARISSIMI.

TETRASTYCHON

REVERENDI LVDOVICI
BATTALEA VENETI.

Audierat muſicos Orpheum, Thamyramq; Linxmq;
Cinthius, & dixit: vincis virumq; Line.

Si Veneta, Claudi, tua tot modulamina in Vrbe
Audiſſet, poſſet dicere: cede Line.

IN

IN OBITV

PERILLVSTRIS, ET ADM. REVERENDI
D. CLAVDII MONTIS VIRIDIS
DIVI MARCI BASILICAE VENETIARVM
MVSICES MODERATORIS EXIMII
TVMVLVS
REVERENDI LVDOVICI
BATTALEA.

..*.*.*

Lacte Cremona aluit, compreſſit Mantua morbo
Extinctum Veneto me tenet arma ſinu.

ALIVS.

Claudius (heu lachrimæ) breniori clauditur vrna
Quam breuibus clauſit verba animata notis .

JN

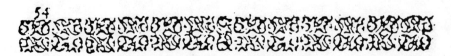

IN LAVDEM

PERILLVSTRIS, ET ADMODVM REVERENDI
D. CLAVDII MONTIS VIRIDIS
IN VENETIARVM DIVI MARCI BASILICA
MVSICORVM PRAEFECTI EXCELLENTISSIMI
HEXASTICON
REVERENDI LODOVICI
BATTALEA.

Pharmaca ne desinit vnquam mortalibus ægris ,
  Musarumq; egeat ne Duce ista cohors .

Altitonante diù secum meditatus in arce
  Iuppiter, hos tandem fudit ab ore sonos :

Humanæ studeat (mandamus) Apollo saluti ,
  Pieridum , Claudi , tu moderere Chorum .

N

IN FVNERE

PERILLVSTRIS, ET ADM. REVERENDI

D. CLAVDII MONTIS VIRIDIS

IN DIVI MARCI VENETIARVM ECCLESIA

MVSICES RECTORIS PRAESTANTISSIMI.

AD CREMONAM HEXASTICON.

REVERENDI LODOVICI BATTALEA.

Claudius en obijt, iacet en quoq; Claudius ille
Cantorum columen, Caſtalidumq; Pater.

Et tu nec lachrymam Genitrix, proh dira Cremona
Sparges? & ſiccas pergis habere genas?

O' feritas : tibi (crede) magis lachrymare liceret,
Quam gemuit Muſicum Thracia priſca ſuum.

DE

56

DE MORTE
CLAVDII MONTE
VERDE.

Olim Mons viridis resonans Virtute canorus.
  Ornauit canux Templa sonora sue.

Spiritus illius Cęli super astra volauit,
  Cum turba Angelica Cantica sacra caxit,

In Terra liquit veram modulaminis Artem,
  Sacratas ędes, quę resonare facit,

Iuppixer ex alto descendit limine Cęli,
  Qualis Apollo nouus police vtroq; canit,

Sic vt Apis prudens, quę mel ex floribus haurit,
  Cantibus ex raris hic meliora capit,

Claudius exiſtat quam vis sub marmore Clausus,
  Nomine perpetuo sic Ioue tonante viget,

Iuppiter iſte sonat Cantus sic nobilis auctor,
  Hinc ęterna sibi Gloria iure venit.

FRAN-

FRANCISCVS RODISEVS.

Vos Aonidum chori, proceres modulaminum
Luctuosa deplorate fata ; & sacros claudite fontes.
Dicite;cur ingemiscens Apollo Lyrã choreis indulgentẽ pessundat ?
Cur Plectrum aureum supra radians genu disrumpit ?
Num Musices phœnix, metri decus, meli numen defecit?
Num canorus concidit Orbis?
Num Mortis gutturnium potuit deglutere montem ?
Musices viriscentia inaruit Monte Viridi siccato:
Ipse Claudius Monsviridis   Harmonicus seraphim:
Eheu clausus, explanatus, exustus, dissonus, aphonus;
Vah voces sine sono, & sine rithmo soni ?
Cecidit, e Cœlo musico in astras Lethes vndas musicus phœton :
Vada illa en clara, defunctisq; canora?
Quis dein obibit inuitus, si Lethe animas rapit?
Vos Brennei Ioris Chori ferales concinite Nęnias,
Et Princeps ille Cantator Incantator Cloti forcipe fatali musici,
ordinis numeros pulset .
Vos Cytharam, barbiton Organum suspendite ad Tumulum,
Ambrosia hunc aspergite, mjrrha litate:
Dum Claudius in Terris non vinus, in Cœlis Diuus,
cantu ætherco, ideali perenniq;
Fato
Cunctos moderatur Orbes.

H   BAL-

BALTHASAR BONIFACIVS.

Monte isto in Viridi cecinit modo Cycnus Aedon
Et cunctę harmonicę quę modulantur aues.

Omnes nunc istę volucres ibi dulce queruntur.
Dulce omnes pariter collacrymantur ibi

Iure dolent, plorant meritò, quia Montis Amœni
Quem falx dira secat, iam Viror omnis abest,

Monte isto in Viridi semper mirabilis Echo
Vocibus haud mutilis integra verba dedit

Quodq; magis miremur adhuc, non illa canendo
Vnisona, aut simplex, sed polyphonos erat

Nunc verò, vt nunquam possit reuirescere posthac
Funditus euersus Mons iacet, illa silet.

Eiusdem,

I N

Excita frondofis Aoniæ lucis funeftas Melpomene
Nenius
Et tragico vincta cothurno, ruentis Muficæ fata
Erato Mecum deplora
Occidit eheu : qui veftros excoleret cœtus
Et
Átropos Inuida
Plectra vobis
Huius filo
Succidit.
Claufus Mons Viridis arida delitefcit Tumba,
Dum
Claudij Monte Verdi clara obmutefcit tuba
Cecinit Cecidit,
Et
Dulci cuncta prius folatus concentu
Duro replet eheu folutus lamento
Expauit lyram Rhadamantus Orphei
Et
Nouos Euridicis raptus
Nouo raptu
intercepit.
Tuderant Eridanus Regia vrna in Regiam Vrbem
Debitum tributi pignus
Vt qui
Nereides amaras óccidens mifcet dulcedine
Thefpiades dulces occidens mifceret amaritudine
Soluite crines
Fundite lachrymas
Scindite purpuras
Spargite cineres
Pangite ; plangite
Piu:n Pyeriæ Patrem,
Quem
Vna veftrum Vrania
Cœleftes inter Mufas
ad fcribat.

H 2   DE

DE MORTE
CLAVDII MONTE
VERDE.

Hei mihi, quid celebris tam Virtus Adepta labore :
Heu, quid delitiç, diuitiçque iuuant .

Heu, quç fatales mortalia fata gubernant
Falce Venenata fila operata secant ;

Is decus Italiæ Cantu mirabile monstrum
Vrna hac frigidior conditur, ecce gelu

Aut pereas æterna, aut Vitç luce fruaris
Vita erit, extremos, viuere obire, dies .

PRO

PRO EXEQVIIS

A IOANNE BAPTISTA MARINONO
IOVE NVNCVPATO,

IN TEMPLO MAGNAE DOMVS VENETIARVM
SOLEMNITER PERACTIS OCCASIONE
OBITVS CLAVDII MONTE VERDE
CREMONENSIS, MVSICI EXCELLENTISSIMI,
AD CAPELLAM
SERENISSIMAE REIPVBLICAE VENETAE
IN SANCTI MARCI
DVCALEM ECCLESIAM PRAEFECTI.

CLAVDIO MONTE VERDE.

ANAGRAMMA

LAVDENT CORDE IOVEM.

ANTONIVS DE EPISCOPIS CLERICVS,
ET CIVIS VENETVS.

Juppiter in Terris surgentem cantat amicum
Nectendo celebri dulcia verba modo ,

Concordes animi fuerant. Quicunque loquuntur
CORDE IOVEM LAVDENT, Claudio amante Iouem.

PRO

PRO OBITV

C L A V D I I   M O N T E   V E R D E

C R E M O N E N S I S

M V S I C I   E X C E L L E N T I S S I M I

A D   C A P E L L A M

S E R E N I S S I M A E   R E I P V B L I C A E   V E N E T A E

I N   D V C A L I   E C C L E S I A   S A N C T I   M A R C I

V E N E T I A R V M   P R A E F E C T I.

C L A V D I O   M O N T E   V E R D E.

A N A G R A M M A

I O V E   C A N T V   M E L   R E D D O.

ANTONIVS DE EPISCOPIS CLERICVS,
ET CIVIS VENETVS.

Noſtro è complexu redeunti Claudio ad aſtra,
CANTV MEL Cordis REDDO iubente IOVE.

VA-

VATICINIVM ARITHMETICVM.

Antonius de Episcopis Clericus, & Ciuis Venetus.

Quis	63
Ascendet	68
In	22
Montem	75
Domini	61
Aut	40
Quis	63
Stabit	68
In	22
Loco	42
Sancto	68
Eius	52
Innocens	88
Manibus	75
Et	24
Mundo	63
Corde	43
Psal.	45
xxiij	69
Ergo	43
Claudius	86
Monteverdi	114
Cremonensis	127
Musicus	100
V.	20
Anno	41
Domini	61
	1643

H V.

MVSÆ PLORANTES DICVNT.

D. ALPHONSVS GRILLOTVS.

*****

Conuersa est lgtitia nostra in luctum, & cantica nostra in planctu.

Generatio nostra laudabit opera tua, & virtutem Canticorum tuorum pronuntiabit.

Erunt Puluis in Terram opera tua in lucem sempiternam Et spiritus ad Deum, qui fecit illum.

MAR.

MARCANTONIVS ROMITVS.

Mons Viridis Terra liquit, Cœlumq; petiuit
Incipiet Cœli dulcius esse Melos.

DE INCISO VITAE STAMINE
CLAVDII MONTIS VIRIDIS

EPIGRAMMA.

Mons Viridis Virtutis fiammæ, gloria cantus
Claudius extremum clausit orbe diem.

Non iactura leuis, lacrymas effundite cuncti,
Non musca, vt vulgò, Musica tota perit.

I   VА.

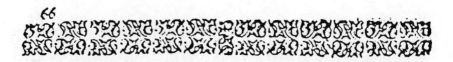

VATICINIVM ARITHMETICVM.

Antonius de Episcopis Clericus, & Ciuis Venetus.

Claudio	62
Monteverde	114
Cremonensis	109
Ad	5
Augumentum	109
Virtutum	176
Peritissimo	123
Harmonie	80
Auxiliatori	131
Ad	5
Superos	85
In	22
Senectute	107
Pia	25
Annorum	58
Lxxv	75
Assumpto	217
Excquie	82
A	1
Ioue	48
Agentur	82
Idem	15
Dcc.	12
An.	14
Dom.	30
	1643

R13

VISIONE RICEVVTA
DELL' ECCELLENTISSIMO
SIGNOR CLAVDIO
MONTE VERDE.

DI D. ALFONSO GRILLOTTI,
Cognominato Targa.

Fuor dell' Alghe marine,
    Il Sol all' Orizonte,
    Apparue il Verde Monte,
    A miei occhi mortali,
    Sormontando con Ali,
    Vnito al Dio di Delo
Così salì, sparì, volante in Cielo.

I 2   50

SOPRA LA MORTE
DELL'ECCELLENTISSIMO
SIGNOR CLAVDIO
MONTEVERDE.

DI D. ALFONSO GRILLO TI,
Cognominato Targa.

Cadè, perche la Parca,
Troncando il fil vitale;
Non guardando à immortale
Delle Muse il Monarca.
Ma il Mondo, il Monte verde,
Se ben l'ombra fuggi, fà che rinuerde
Nè cangiarà suo fine,
Sin che non fia il Pastor vn sol Quile.

69

IN LODE
DELL' ECCELLENTISSIMO CLAVDIO
MONTE VERDE,
NEL FVNERAL.

Stupisce huomeni , e belue ,
  Dal grato suon d' vna Canora Cetra ,
  (O merauiglia tetra ,)
  Si mouesser le selue ,
  Maggior stupor quest' hora
  Poi ch' hor il verde moue ,
  Con sue palese proue
  Collegio musicabil ; che l' honora ,
  D' vn premio di Corona
  D' vn verdeggiante suon , Che Gioue Dona .

ALL' ISTESSO.

Tra le più scielte schiere
  De Musici gentil Cigni Canori
  Claudio l' honor de Chori
  Trasse col dolce Canto huomeni , e fiere ;
  Monte già verde , hor horrida , e sfiorita ,
  Terra , le pietre à ricoprirlo muita .

Bernardo Moscatello.

IN

IN MORTE DI CLAVDIO MONTEVERDE.

SONETTO MVSICALE, DEL PADRE MAESTRO PAVLO PIAZZA.

E' la pena, il godimento .

la vita de' mortali,

la virtù trà tanti mali

più la pompa, e 'l vento,

Sdrucciola, come ogni contento,

Qual leggier il giorno hà l'alti

Non mai han ò quiete i dì vitali

acuto graue ogni momento ;

Il contrapunto delle humane attioni
E' finger, alterar, cader. falire
Capricci, fantafie, Giri, Inuentioni,

Scherzi, Brilli, Correnti, paci, ed ire,
Paffaggi, affetti, fughe, e mutationi,
Di tal Mufica è il Morire.

P. P.

IL FINE.

AL LETTORE.

AVuerti , Lettore , che in mirando le ſudette Compoſitioni con occhio maligno , la lingua non dica , che bene : Poiche gl'Auttori , ſe vi ſcorgi errori , non gl'hanno commeſſi ; mà ſono mancamenti per non hauer hauuto Cenſore , che gli aſſiſti .

Bibliography

Books and Music Prior to 1700

Agazzari, Agostino. *Del suonare sopra'l Basso*. Siena: Domenico Falcini, 1607.

Banchieri, Adriano. *Eclesiastiche Sinfonie*. Venetia: Amadino, 1607.

Boschini, Marco. *La Carta del Navegar Pitoresco*. Venezia: Baba, 1660.

Bottrigari, Ercole. *Il Desiderio*. Venezia: Ricciardo Amadino, 1594.

Grillo, Angelo. *Dalle lettere*. Venezia: Evangelista Deuchino, 1616.

Grillo, Angelo. *Pietosi affetti*. Venezia: Giunti e Ciotti, 1608.

Maugars, André. *Response faite a un curieux sur le sentiment de la Musique d'It..lie*. Paris: 1639.

Sansovino, Francesco. *Venetia città nobilissima*. Edited by Giustinian Martinio.. Venezia: Stefano Curti, 1663.

Strozzi, Giulio. *I cinque fratelli*. Venezia: Deuchino, 1628.

Vecchi, Orazio. *Selva di varia recreatione*. Venezia: Angelo Gardano, 1590.

Viadana, Lodovico. *Salmi a quattro cori*. Venezia: Vincenti, 1612.

Modern Publications

Arnold, Denis. "Monteverdi's Church Music: Some Venetian Traits." *Monthly sical Record* 83 (1958): 83–91.

Askew, Pamela. "Fetti's 'Portrait of an Actor' Reconsidered." *The Burling Magazine* 120 (1978): 59.

Blackburn, Bonnie J., and Edward E. Lowinsky. "Luigi Zenobi and His Lette the Perfect Musician." *Studi Musicali* 22 (1993): 61.

Fabbri, Paolo. "Inediti Monteverdiani." *Rivista Italiana di Musicologia* 15 (19 71.

Ferand, Ernst T. "Die Motetti, Madrigali, et Canzoni Francese . . . des Gio Bassano (1591)," in *Festschrift Helmuth Osthoff*. Tutzing: 1961.

Glixon, Jonathan. "Was Monteverdi a Traitor?" *Music and Letters* 72 (199

Gurlitt, Willibald. "Ein Briefwechsel zwischen Paul Hainlein und L. Frie haim aus den Jahren 1647–48." *Sammelbände der Internationalen Mi schaft* 14 (1912–13): 481.

Huyghens, Constantijn. "Journal van zijne Reis naar Venetie in 1620. en Mededeelingen van het Historisch Genootschap* 15 (1894): 128

)nterosso, Raffaello. *Una firma autografa di Marco Ingegneri in un documento 'nedito.* Cremona: 1946.

)nteverdi, Claudio. *Lettere: edizione critica a cura di Eva Lax.* Florence: 1994.

———. *Letters.* Revised edition by Denis Stevens. Oxford: 1995.

)ore, James H. *"Venezia favorita da Maria:* Music for the Madonna Nicopeia and Santa Maria della Salute." *Journal of the American Musicological Society* 34 (1981): 249.

ntiroli, Giuseppe. "Notizie di musicisti cremonesi dei secoli XVI," *Bollettino Storico Cremonese* 22 (1961–64): 169.

anders, Steven. "The Hapsburg Court of Ferdinand II and the *Messa, Magnificat et Iubilate Deo a sette chori concertati con le trombe* (1621) of Giovanni Valentini," *Journal of the American Musicological Society* 44 (1991): 359.

Ifridge-Field, Eleanor. *Venetian Instrumental Music from Gabrieli to Vivaldi.* Oxford: 1975.

Index